WITHDRAWN

11/00

Obesity

Obesity

Look for these and other books in the Lucent Overview Series:

Obesity

by Charlene Akers

Lucent
Books

Library of Congress Cataloging-in-Publication Data

Akers, Charlene
    Obesity / by Charlene Akers.
        p.   cm. — (Lucent overview series)
Includes bibliographical references and index.
Summary: Discusses various definitions of obesity and its possible
causes, consequences, treatment, and prevention.
    ISBN 1-56006-662-8 (lib. bdg. : alk. paper)
    1. Obesity—Juvenile literature. [1. Obesity] I. Title.
    II. Series.
RC628 . A356 2000
616.3'98—dc21   99-046398

Copyright © 2000 by Lucent Books, Inc.
P.O. Box 289011, San Diego, CA 92198-9011
Printed in the U.S.A.

Contents

Introduction

OBESITY IS AN escalating epidemic of alarming proportions and one of the most severe health problems in the United States. Since 1980, when the number of overweight Americans hovered at about 25 percent, weights among Americans have soared. Now more than half of the population is overweight and nearly one-quarter of adult Americans are considered obese.

The U.S. government, under the auspices of the National Center for Health Statistics, has been collecting information on obesity in America since 1960. Over the forty years since then, four nationwide surveys have gathered statistics on weight. The sampling process was thorough, and the surveys are thought to be representative of the U.S. population across all ages, income strata, and ethnic groups.

The first survey, completed in 1962, showed that almost 13 percent of the population was obese. The next two surveys, completed in 1974 and 1980, revealed only a moderate increase in the rate of obesity. The fourth survey, however, completed in 1994, showed that the percentage of overweight Americans had increased dramatically. Some 55 percent of all Americans were officially considered overweight, and 35 percent of adult Americans were classified as obese, meaning that people in this group weighed 20 percent more than their ideal weight, given their height, gender, and age.

Who is obese?

Researchers found that no group in the nation was spared by the epidemic of obesity. The increase in obesity

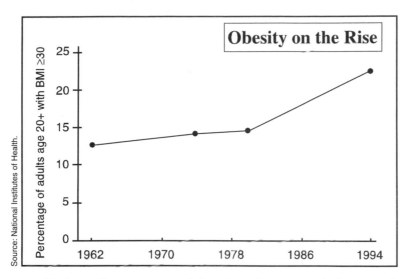

applied to all segments of the American population. Both men and women were affected, regardless of age, ethnicity, or level of education.

Although no group of Americans is immune to obesity, some are affected to a greater degree. Broken down by gender, race, and ethnicity, the data varied tremendously. For example, 39 percent of Mexican American men were found to be obese while the percentage for black men was 32 and for white men 31. Statistics show that nearly half of all African American women (48.5 percent) and Mexican American women (47 percent) are obese as opposed to a third of white women (32 percent). Overall, obese women outnumbered obese men, but only by a single percentage point. Researchers believe that these variations are determined by a combination of cultural and demographic factors.

One alarming statistic is the increase in obesity among adolescents. In the period between 1976 and 1980, 15 percent of adolescents aged twelve to nineteen were obese. By the next survey (1988–1991), the figure had jumped to 21 percent, a 40 percent increase.

Even children have been affected by the obesity epidemic. Between 1980 and 1994, the number of obese children in the United states almost doubled, with nearly 14 percent of all children six to eleven now considered overweight. Such findings suggest that the problem of obesity is affecting Americans sooner; therefore, if left untreated, obesity has more time to harm its victims.

More than just a cosmetic problem

While being overweight is often considered a cosmetic problem, obesity is also a financial and public health burden. The financial costs to the nation are estimated to exceed $68 billion a year in direct and indirect expenses such as doctor bills and time missed from work. Evidence shows that obesity is the second-leading cause of death in the United States, after smoking, and is directly responsible for a large portion of heart disease, cancer, and diabetes.

While experts agree on its devastating consequences, they continue to disagree on whether genetic or environmental factors are more responsible for causing obesity. Heredity appears to play a role in determining both body type and an individual's propensity to put on weight, but environmental factors seem to be even more

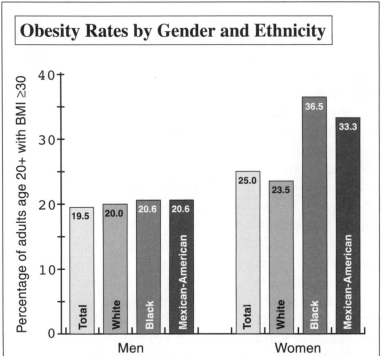

Obesity Rates by Gender and Ethnicity

Source: National Institutes of Health, 1994.

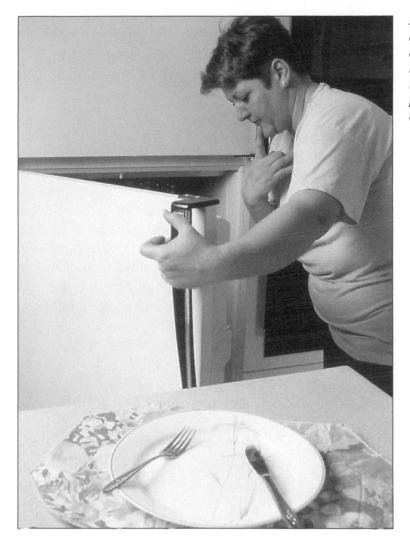

Although genetics play a role in a person's ability to maintain a healthy weight, obesity is attributed mostly to poor diet and lack of exercise.

influential. Increased availability of cheap, calorie-dense food and decreased levels of exercise are probably more to blame for the meteoric rise in obesity than genetics. The United States has about 215,000 fast-food restaurants, and government statistics show that 45 percent of the U.S. food budget is spent for meals and snacks eaten away from home. To make matters worse, more than half of all adult Americans get no regular physical activity, and 25 percent get none at all. The extent of obesity in the United States is a sobering reminder of the negative consequences of prosperity and the technological advances that occurred in the later half of the twentieth century.

Besides disagreement over its causes, controversy also rages about the most effective way to treat obesity. Lacking any firm guidance on how obesity can be treated, Americans spend more than $33 billion a year on products and services designed to help them shed unwanted pounds. The most remarkable feature of the thousands of treatments, devices, therapies, programs, and products that promise weight loss is their rate of failure. Some even result in significant health risks. Given the ineffectiveness of most weight-loss treatments, the solution to America's obesity crisis must be found in prevention. Therefore, experts are turning their attention to helping Americans establish healthy eating and exercise habits.

1

The Moving Target: Defining Obesity

OBESITY IS A condition of excess fatness that results from an imbalance between energy consumed and energy expended. In other words, when the human body takes in more food than it uses up, the extra is stored in fat deposits, resulting in increased weight. But *obesity* is a relative term. Any definition of *obesity* is arbitrary and subject to shifts in

Obesity is difficult to define because the term is subject to shifts in fashion.

perceptions, both on the part of health experts and the general public. Dr. F. Xavier Pi-Sunyer, one of the country's leading experts on obesity, points out that determining whether someone is obese depends on a number of factors:

> A population cannot be precisely divided into normal and obese. . . . In the modern world, with the great intermixing of ethnic and racial groups, wide genetic heterogeneity exists. The heterogeneity is manifested by differing heights, body circumference (chest, waist, hips,) and heaviness of frame. It is undesirable to focus on a single number as the "normal" weight. This is particularly evident since it is not clear what the criterion for "normal" weight should be.[1]

Shifting fashions in beauty

Since the beginning of the twentieth century, health professionals in America have searched for a way to define obesity using numerical values. But for most Americans, whether someone was considered obese had more to do with fashion than with physical health or life expectancy. In fact, in earlier times fatness was regarded as a sign of good health as well as beauty and affluence.

Historically, obesity was seen as proof that a person could get enough to eat. Until modern machinery and improved agricultural techniques made the growing, preserving, and transporting of food easier, simply getting enough to eat was a constant struggle for many people. As visible proof of the triumph over hunger, fatness was equated with success. Accordingly, thinness was considered a sign of failure and was not only equated with poor health but was also considered unattractive for both men and women.

Just as fashions change in clothing and hairstyles, so does the idea of what constitutes obesity and whether it is desirable. In the 1870s the voluptuous figure was the American ideal for women. The attraction of fat was further supported by a medical theory that equated plumpness with health. Many doctors recommended that both men and women should try to keep their weight up. Some doctors went so far as to argue that the production of a large number of fat cells was crucial to a well-balanced personality. In 1895, for example, one health magazine praised the social reformer Elizabeth Cady Stanton for "that plumpness which indicates superb health, and it would be difficult to find a more perfect sign of digestion than is shown in the fullness of her cheeks."[2] Stanton, who by today's standards would be considered decidedly obese, represented the ideal image of a woman of her times

As is true today, famous people helped set standards of appearance for the rest of the nation. For the last two decades of the nineteenth century, the actress Lillian Russell was considered synonymous with female beauty. In her day the most photographed woman in America, Lillian Russell at her peak tipped the scales at 250 pounds. "A golden-haired goddess with big rounded cheeks, soft and dimpled like a baby's," she was "an edition of deluxe femininity."[3] Her love of gargantuan meals insured there was plenty of her to see.

Not until the late 1800s when America shifted from an agricultural economy to an industrial one did these views change. Large numbers of people gave up farming and moved to the cities to work in factories, offices, and shops. They no longer grew their own food on small farms but bought what they needed to eat in stores. As food became more accessible and convenient the majority of people could get enough to eat. When it became possible for almost anyone to get the food they needed and more, obesity ceased to be a sign of wealth and success.

The voluptuous American actress Lillian Russell was once considered the ideal of beauty. In today's society many would consider her overweight.

As the nineteenth century drew to a close America's ideal began to shift from the rounded full figure as exemplified in Lillian Russell's hefty proportions to a new lithe slimness. In 1896, after a newspaper review compared her to a white elephant, even Lillian Russell went on a diet. The popularity of the voluptuous figure was in decline and a new standard of beauty was on the rise.

Representing the transition from fat to thin was the Gibson Girl, creation of the artist Charles Dana Gibson. In advertisements the Gibson Girl became the new American ideal. Still large by today's standards, with broad shoulders, large breasts, wide hips and a slender waist, she represented a new ideal body type—strong, healthy, athletic. Gibson girls were pictured riding bicycles, playing tennis, golf, croquet, and engaging in many outdoor activities.

American women responded to the changing ideal by making changes in their own bodies. As more women began attending college, working outside the home, and participating in sports, the ideal woman became thinner and more athletic. Whereas less-endowed women had once resorted to padding both their bust and hips to achieve the desired hourglass figure, they now began binding their breasts to approximate the boyish shape that was the new feminine ideal. By the 1920s, thin was in. According to one writer,

The Gibson Girl helped change the public's notion of the ideal figure from voluptuous to more slender and athletic.

In the 1920's for the first time, teen age girls made systematic efforts to lower their weight by food reduction and exercise. College girls in the 1920's worked hard to become slender. Instead of writing home happily about weight gain and abundant eating, as female collegians had done in the 1880's and 1890's, young women debated the virtues of different diet plans and worried about gaining weight.[4]

The trend toward thinness

Women strove for the new slender figure featured in fashion magazines, movies, and advertisements. Medical professionals changed their tune as well as far as women were concerned, at least. Doctors warned of the dangers of being overweight, and women began to do whatever they could to be slim. One writer notes of the time,

> They starved themselves and chewed gum laced with laxatives to lose weight. Told to Reach for a Lucky instead of a sweet, they took up smoking to lose weight; it was, as the ad said, "the modern way to diet." They followed a number of wild fad diets recommended by physicians and pseudophysicians, many of which involved fasting, purgatives, and odd combinations of foods.[5]

From the 1920s on, the ideal for American women became thinner and thinner. In 1947 the French fashion designer Christian Dior introduced "the New Look," featuring dresses with full skirts and tiny waists that women had to become even thinner to squeeze into. "We wondered where in the world we were going to get models who could get into them," remembers a woman who was a model when the new fashion began to take hold. "Then out of the woods came these nymphs with no lungs and very little of the flesh that keeps you alive. These new kids really don't eat."[6]

A review of fashion magazines published since the forties shows the increasing slenderness of fashion models, culminating in the 1960s with the supermodel Lesley Hornsby, popularly known as Twiggy, who carried no more than ninety-nine pounds on her five-foot six-inch frame. Since Twiggy's day, models have become taller and more muscular while remaining extremely thin, even

An increase in advertisements for fat-reducing products and the circulation of fad diets in the late 1800s reflected a trend toward thinness in the public's perception of beauty.

Don't Be Too Fat

Don't ruin your stomach with a lot of useless drugs and patent medicines. Send to Prof. F. J. Kellogg, 1366 W. Main St., Battle Creek, Michigan, for a free trial package of a treatment that will reduce your weight to normal without diet or drugs. The treatment is perfectly safe, natural and scientific. It takes off the big stomach, gives the heart freedom, enables the lungs to expand naturally, and you will feel a hundred times better the first day you try this wonderful home treatment.

gaunt. For many American women, the exceptionally thin and toned body of the supermodel has become the ideal body type of today.

Ironically, Americans keep getting fatter even as their ideal body type keeps getting thinner. The obsession with thinness can be observed in fashion magazines and the advertising in other periodicals, as well as in the proliferation of diets and diet books. Until 1950, articles dealing with weight reduction were almost unknown in popular American publications: between 1937 and 1945 there were fewer than two per year. But in the late 1990s, it is a rare woman's magazine that doesn't feature at least one article about the latest way to lose weight or offer fashion spreads with models clad in the latest styles designed to make the wearer look thin.

The 1960s model Lesley Hornsby, known as Twiggy, signaled the advent of super thin and toned figures as the ideal body type.

Even the icons of American advertising have slimmed down over the years. The once comfortably plump Aunt Jemima is now fashionably trim; Psyche, White Rock Beverage's beautiful winged symbol, who weighed a voluptuous 140 pounds in the 1880s, was reduced to a neat 118 pounds in the 1980s. Even the chubby Campbell soup kids have lost some of their baby fat. Wherever they look, Americans are bombarded with the message that thin is best.

A new concern for men

The period between the 1890s and the 1920s in America saw the transition from plump to thin as the preferred body type, at least for women. The aesthetic standards for masculine beauty took longer to change. Although obesity as a health problem looms as large for men as it does for women, historically much less attention has been paid to obesity as an aesthetic concern for men. As one writer points out,

> A man with substantial bulk commanded respect. He possessed what was called a "noble" waistline. If a lot of the weight was fat, so much the better. It was tangible proof that he could not only acquire enough food to stay alive—he could acquire *more* than enough. Being fat meant that a man was successful. And tangible evidence of success, just as it currently does, guarantees a man's social acceptance. Until quite recently, a man's fatness was of no great significance as far as his personal appearance was concerned, except in extreme cases. Other men did not especially care how he looked. If anything, bulk gave the impression of power and sexual vigor even if much of size consisted of fat. The opposite sex was more interested in a man's ability to be a provider than anything else. As a fat man, he had conspicuous evidence that he was an able provider.[7]

It was not until late in the twentieth century that men started being bombarded with the message that thinness matters. Advertisements featuring half-naked young men with washboard stomachs and magazines devoted to bodybuilding and muscle development began setting a new standard for men's looks. One psychoanalyst who counsels patients dealing with obesity notes that men are starting to respond to the pressure to be attractive in the same way that women have for years. "The image of beauty is out there and one tries to match or compare oneself to that image. Today there is much more heightened consciousness about appearance. If you come up short, it's a problem."[8]

As the ideal body type grew progressively thinner for both men and women, Americans began to concern themselves with the numbers they read on the bathroom scale. Until the end of the nineteenth century, nobody thought much about weight and whether a person could weigh too much. True, members of the clergy had in the past preached against the sin of gluttony on moral grounds, but their concern was spiritual rather than physical health. But as American culture began to idealize thinness, both the health profession and the general public began to concern themselves with defining what constituted the ideal weight for everyone.

Today men face some of the same pressures as women to stay thin in order to be attractive.

Ideal-weight tables

In 1943 the Metropolitan Life Insurance Company (MetLife) published the Height-Weight Mortality Ratio Tables, which showed the ideal body weight for men and women depending on their height. For each listed measurement in height, an ideal weight range of thirty pounds was shown. Louis Dublin, the insurance company executive who created the charts, later narrowed the ideal weight range from about thirty pounds to about ten pounds. Since their publication, the MetLife tables have been the standard for determining if a person is obese. Many doctors consider patients obese if they weigh 20 percent more than their ideal weight as listed in the tables.

As their name suggests, the insurance tables are based on the assumption that people who weigh within a certain range are less likely to die at an early age than people who weigh more (or less) than this range. At first glance, that assumption seems valid. But the data used for constructing the tables are not representative of the American public as a whole. The information is based on data gathered by insurance companies about their policyholders. The problem is that since not everyone has health insurance, most of the information on which the tables are based comes from a select group: policyholders who are white middle-class men between the ages of twenty-five and fifty-nine. As Dr. Mavis Thompson explains,

> The tables may be accurate for other middle-class white males in this age range, but whether they are valid for a huge segment of the population including African-Americans and other persons of color, not to mention women, children, teens, young adults and adults past middle age is a matter of recent debate. For years doctors assumed that obesity and other conditions that were risky for white males posed the same health hazard to everyone else. That may be true in some cases, but until scientists study other population groups—female and male, African-Americans and other races alike—as carefully as they've studied white males, it will be difficult to say for sure. Obesity and other conditions that pose a health problem for white males may not be a hazard for other groups.[9]

In response to concerns about the lack of diversity in the insurance company's samples, the federal government published its own weight tables in 1990. The government's tables increase the range of ideal weight, making it possible for a person to weigh more than the ideal weight indicated on the Metropolitan Life tables without being classified as obese. Taking into consideration the fact that people tend to get heavier as they get older, the government's tables also make allowances for increased weight in people above the age of thirty-five.

Body Mass Index

Despite the government's efforts to make it easier to compare weights among a diverse population, researchers looked for a more precise measurement of obesity. In the late 1980s the Body Mass Index (BMI) replaced the Metropolitan Life ideal-weight charts as the preferred method among experts for determining obesity. Originally proposed by the mathematician Lambert Adolphe Jacques Quételet in 1871, the BMI is considered more precise than the MetLife tables and an easy way to compare the fatness of people of different heights regardless of gender. The BMI, the ratio of weight to the square of height, is found by dividing the person's body weight in kilograms by the square of the person's height in meters: $BMI = (weight)/(height)^2$. The BMI may also be determined by multiplying weight in pounds by 700, then dividing this figure by height in inches and dividing this figure again by height in inches: $BMI = (weight\ in\ pounds) \times (700)/(height\ in\ inches)^2$. For example, to find the BMI of someone five feet ten inches tall and weighing 185 pounds, the calculations are as follows:

$$185\ pounds \times 700 = 129,500$$
$$129,500 \div 70\ inches = 1,850$$
$$1,850 \div 70\ inches = 26.4$$

When the BMI was introduced, the cutoff point for being considered obese was 30. That is, anyone with a BMI above 30 was rated as obese. In June 1998, after an extensive review of the scientific literature on obesity showed that the risk of an early death increases when a BMI of 27 or 28 is reached, the National Institutes of Health (NIH) issued new guidelines, which lowered the acceptable BMI from 30 to 25. Under the revised guidelines, a BMI between 19 and 25 falls within the healthy range (19 to 23 for men, 22 to 25 for women.) A BMI between 26 and 29 is considered overweight, and 30 or over is morbidly obese. By the new definition, a person with a BMI of 25 or 26 is now considered overweight. A man or a woman five feet seven inches tall and weighing 159 pounds who before would have been within the healthy range with a BMI of 25, is now considered overweight.

Like the MetLife tables and government weight tables, the BMI has drawbacks as a measure of obesity. Because lean muscle tissue weighs more than fat, a person with overdeveloped muscles can have a high BMI and still not be obese. For example, a six-foot tall, 275-pound football player would be considered obese by the charts and government guidelines. But, as a professional athlete, he would probably be very muscular and have very little body fat. Because the extra weight is muscle, he would not be obese. On the other hand, a man six feet tall weighing 184 pounds who gets no exercise would be well within the normal range with a BMI of 25 even though he is carrying too much fat.

Fat distribution—too heavy or too fat?

Increasingly, experts believe that body fat, and particularly where the fat is located on the body, may be more important than weight in determining obesity. According to the NIH, a healthy body fat measurement is 23 percent or

BMI Guidelines	
Classification	Body Mass Index
Underweight	less than 18.5
Normal	18.5 – 24.9
Overweight	25.0 – 29.9
Obese	30.0 – 39.9
Extremely Obese	40.0 or higher

Source: National Institutes of Health.

less for women and 18 percent or less for men. For example, if a man weighs 150 pounds and has 10 percent body fat, it means that his frame is made up of 135 pounds of lean tissue and 15 pounds of fatty tissue. The problem, then, is how to determine body fat.

There are a number of body-fat tests, but the three most common are the skin-fold, bioelectrical impedance, and underwater weighing. In the skin-fold test, calipers measure the thickness of the fat in several areas, such as the abdomen, thighs, hips, and backs of the arms. The measurements are then plugged into a formula to determine the body-fat percentage. The disadvantage of this technique is that the measurement itself is difficult to make precisely. A measurement one inch off the right spot can cause an inaccurate reading and throw off the calculations.

The bioelectrical impedance test is much more reliable than the skin-fold test, but it requires more specialized equipment. Electrodes are attached to the hand, wrist, foot, or ankle and a current is sent through the body. Fat-free tissue is a better conductor of electrical current than fatty tissue is, so the lower the electrical impedance reading, the lower the percentage of a person's weight that is attributed to fat.

The most accurate measure of body fat is underwater weighing. This test weighs a person while submerged in water. Though regarded by experts as the most accurate means of body-fat testing, the necessary equipment is not available in most physicians' offices. Moreover, the equations developed to determine the body fat by this means were based solely on measurements conducted on males ages twenty to forty. Thus, the measurement suffers from some of the same disadvantages as the ideal-weight tables.

Not only do most techniques for calculating body fat require sophisticated equipment not always available in a doctor's office, but many health professionals believe that it is body-fat distribution, not weight or the ratio of fat to lean tissue, that is most useful in determining who is obese.

An easy and accurate indication of fat distribution is the Waist/Hip Ratio (WHR), which is simply a person's waist measurement divided by the hip measurement. For women

A skin-fold test is performed on a patient to determine the percentage of body fat.

a ratio of 0.8 or less is preferred, meaning that their hips ought to be 25 percent larger than their waistline. Men are considered healthiest if their hips and waistlines are roughly equal, with a WHR of .95 to 1.0.

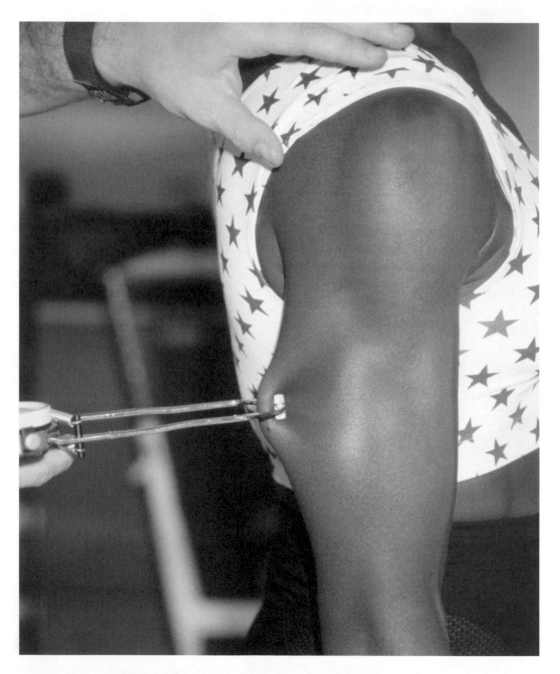

   Public opinion continues to redefine the perception of who is too fat on an ever-shifting aesthetic scale, and scientists are working to refine the tools that will help them find an accurate measurement of obesity. Meanwhile, researchers and health professionals are searching for a better understanding of what causes obesity.

2

The Puzzle of Obesity: An Elusive Cause

EVERYONE AGREES THAT obesity results when more calories are taken in than are used up. A debate rages, however, between people who cite environmental factors as the cause of obesity and those who claim heredity is to blame. Moreover, no one understands completely why some people can eat a lot and never gain an ounce while others eat much less and get fat. Proponents of the environmental side of the argument suggest that, except for very rare genetic diseases, people get fat because they overeat. Those on the heredity side of the debate argue that people with a genetic tendency to obesity will weigh more than the accepted norm no matter how much they exercise and how carefully they watch their calorie intake.

What is fat?

Although scientists have not yet come to an agreement on what makes people fat, they do have a clear understanding of the properties and origin of body fat. The fat stored in the body comes from the food a person consumes, and it does not matter if the food is in the form of protein, carbohydrates, or fat itself. When a person eats more food than the body needs to produce energy or build tissue, the liver converts the excess into fat that is stored in specialized cells.

Most of the 30 million fat cells in the average human body accumulate in loose connective tissue between the organs, various muscle groups, and groups of bone and muscle that hold the body together. This loose connective tissue is called adipose tissue.

A matter of fat distribution

Although individuals differ in the amount and distribution of adipose tissue, most human beings fall into one of

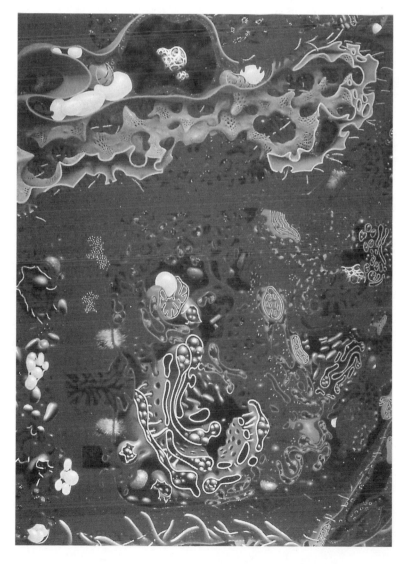

Liver cells convert excess energy to fat, which is then stored throughout the body, mostly in adipose tissue.

three large categories according to their tendency to store fat and the general amount and location of adipose tissue. The categories were identified in the 1930s by a researcher named William Sheldon. According to Sheldon's system, people can be divided into three basic body types: endomorphs, mesomorphs, and ectomorphs. Endomorphs are characterized by a soft, rounded, fat-covered body. Mesomorphs, characterized by strong, thick bones and large muscles, have stocky, powerful bodies. Ectomorphs, who tend to be thin and delicate with long bones, are the exact opposite of endomorphs.

Although there are variations within each classification, experts who believe that obesity is an inherited trait argue that certain body types are destined to be obese. For example, endomorphs, who seem to gain weight just by looking at food, would have to endure a lifetime of starvation to avoid being considered obese. Ectomorphs, on the other hand, seem to be able to eat constantly and never gain an ounce.

The argument for environment

Although there is evidence that one's body type is inherited, many researchers say that Americans are obese because they just eat too much. "It's what I call the 3,700-calorie-a-day-problem," says nutrition expert Marion Nestle.

> The department of Agriculture reports that the American food supply produced 3,700 calories a day for every man, woman and child in the country. Women need only half that number of calories and men need two thirds of that. But people are constantly bombarded with advertisements that encourage them to eat far more than they need. Advertising budgets for food that no one needs are astronomical.[10]

In other words, there is more food available than people need, but they eat it anyway. In restaurants, for instance, portions have gotten so big that people have a distorted view of what a normal-size portion should be. Journalist Florence Fabricant notes sardonically, "In some restaurants it takes a salvage vessel to recover a fork that accidentally slips into a bowl of fish stew. There are tables set with wine glasses large enough to hold half a bottle. Mega-muffins have become the norm. A pretzel from a street vendor is as much food as five slices of bread."[11]

An unhealthy trend

The trend is for ever-larger portions. The original McDonald's hamburger weighed in at a paltry 3.7 ounces. Now customers can select the 7.6-ounce Big Mac, the 9-ounce Arch Deluxe, or the double Big Mac with four beef patties. Moreover, the extra-large bargain meals offered by many fast-food restaurants encourage patrons to eat even more. According to one writer, "Food and drink portions have ballooned to the point that marketers need a whole new vocabulary to describe them. Selections no longer stop at large. They're jumbo or supreme. They're monster. They're super-size."[12]

It is easy for people to forget that while they get more food for their money, they

The general increase in the size of food portions in the United States is partially blamed for the increase in obesity.

also get more calories and fat. For example, a small order of fries at McDonald's has 210 calories and 10 grams of fat, but the supersize fries have 540 calories and 26 grams of fat. Faced with the chance to more than double the size of an order for a small additional price, many customers yield to the temptation.

Besides increasing the amount of food they eat, Americans are also increasing the number of calories they consume in the form of beverages. According to the National Research Council, one of the most striking changes in eating patterns in the past twenty years has been the increased consumption of soft drinks, citrus juice, beer, and wine. For example, the consumption of carbonated soft drinks went from 19 gallons per person in 1965 to 52 gallons per

A growth in the consumption of beverages like soft drinks and beer has further contributed to an increase in the amount of calories consumed and may be a factor in obesity.

person in 1994, an increase of 140 percent. As with food, soft drink portions are getting larger, contributing to the upward trend. In the late 1960s, for instance, Coca Cola came in a 6.5-ounce bottle and amounted to less than 100 calories. In recent years, machines that dispense 12-ounce cans with 140 calories have become the norm, and some machines offer even larger bottles.

Where the calories originate

Not only are Americans eating and drinking more, but they are also eating more of the wrong things. Recently, attention has been focused on the role of fat in the American diet (Americans on average derive 34 percent of their calories from fat). Protein, carbohydrates, and fat are interchangeable as far as metabolism is concerned, and there is no conclusive evidence that changing the relative proportions of protein, carbohydrates, and fat in one's diet without decreasing total consumption of calories will prevent obesity. However, because fat has a very high calorie count per unit of volume, eating fatty foods promotes the consumption of calories. For example, a gram of fat has nine calories while a gram of carbohydrates has only four. As one doctor explains,

> Fat calories really sneak up on you. A few handfuls of potato chips has the same number of calories as two medium-sized baked potatoes topped with nonfat yogurt and steamed vegetables. Unlike carbohydrates, fat calories don't cause feelings of fullness, so you keep eating and eating, gaining weight and increasing your risk of all the fat-related diseases.[13]

But calories lurk in every food. Despite the fact that the average fat intake has decreased from 36 to 34 percent of the American diet, the total number of calories consumed has increased from an average of 1,969 calories per person per day to 2,200. Often, consumers fail to realize that many products marketed as low fat or fat free have the same number of calories as the regular version because the fat has been replaced by sugar. While many dieters have decreased their dietary fat, they have increased their total

calories, indulging, for instance, in a second or even a third bagel because they're using nonfat cream cheese or downing an entire box of cookies in one sitting because they are nonfat.

One best-selling author of books on dieting notes that low-fat foods lure people into increasing consumption:

> A recent study at the University of California showed that people who were given what they thought was nonfat yogurt ate twice as much as the people given yogurt labeled as containing fat. When we think something doesn't have fat, we fool ourselves into believing it doesn't count, and we eat more than we usually would. Which means we are getting fat on nonfat foods. Since this latest nonfat craze, Americans have gained an average of eight pounds.[14]

Too little exercise

Although Americans are undoubtedly eating more, researchers generally attribute most of the increase in obesity to simple lack of exercise. As Dr. F. Xavier Pi-Sunyer explains, "Somehow in the 1980s, the thinking goes, the effects of modernization—of computers, remote controls, and one or more cars in every garage—combined with an unprecedented abundance of cheap, energy-dense food to produce a population that eats more while becoming ever less physically active."[15] As suburbs have expanded, more and more people rely on their cars for going shopping and running errands. Since increasing numbers of Americans are commuting to work, they are spending hours sitting in a train, bus, or car.

At the same time, the nature of work itself has changed, and all kinds of laborsaving devices mean that people expend less physical energy on the job. One doctor specializing in obesity notes, "During most of this century this was a country in which your work obliged you to be physically active. Now, we can't even get up and go down the hall to deliver a message. We have to send an e-mail."[16]

Laborsaving devices have an impact on many aspects of American life besides work. Dr. Jeffery Koplan, who heads the U.S. Centers for Disease Control and Prevention, points out that modern conveniences designed to save time have also eliminated opportunities to burn calories:

> Unfortunately, movement of everything but the fingers is gradually being engineered out of American life. Walk through your house and think about everything that's been changed. The automatic garage door opener, the cordless phone, the television remote. Everything's electric. Rolling down the windows in your car—you name it. Everything has been motorized or electrified.[17]

Individually, laborsaving devices don't add up to much, but together they play an important role in the obesity problem.

Labor- and timesaving devices themselves are not necessarily bad, but the way that such saved time is used may present a problem. In 1993, 60 percent of Americans were either completely inactive or irregularly active, meaning they exercised fewer than two times a week. A 1996 survey revealed that one- quarter of all Americans do not engage in any physical activity whatsoever during their leisure time. Another survey showed that Americans watch 1,539 hours of television, 51 hours of videos, and play 21 hours of video games a year. That's close to 4.5 hours per day spent sitting in front of a television screen.

Advancements of technology are yet another reason for an increase in obesity.

In particular, television has been cited as the number one cause of childhood and adolescent obesity. Studies show that the more television a child watches, the more likely he or she is to be obese. Most experts agree that the resulting lack of physical activity is the primary reason kids become overweight. Many children simply aren't moving their bodies enough to burn off the calories they take in. According to one of the country's leading obesity researchers,

> Twenty years ago, parents would send their children outside after school, where they'd play hopscotch and climb trees

until dinnertime. Today they're inside playing video games or watching TV. The difference is significant, caloriewise. A child who spends 60 minutes in front of the television will burn 60 calories; a child playing outside (running around, riding a bike) for an hour burns over 200. And kids watching TV, most notably in the after-school hours, are also exposed to a multitude of irresistible commercials featuring high-calorie foods which may prompt them to snack.[18]

Psychological causes of overeating

Some causes of obesity, such as oversized portions and lack of exercise, are, to some extent, controllable. Mental health professionals, however, believe that when people overeat to the point of causing obesity, the reasons are more complex than simple lack of willpower. Instead of listening to signals that tell them they are full, compulsive overeaters eat in response to emotions such as anxiety, anger, fear, sadness, and boredom. Overeating of this sort is often a behavior learned in childhood, when parents used food as a reward or to soothe pain. One compulsive overeater remembers, "I was inadvertently taught that treats cured every 'ouch,' candy soothed every hurt feeling. And if one cookie made you feel good, five made you delirious with joy."[19]

Researcher Sonia Caprio notes that parents often contribute less directly to their children's obesity:

> How parents relate to their children also affects youngsters' ways of dealing with food. A child who has never had limits set may never have learned when to stop watching television or when to stop eating. When a child is indulged he or she learns unhealthy habits. Yet when one or both parents are distant and a child is not nurtured and supported, the child may seek out food as comfort in order to feel better. In this case a child may well be trying to fill a void.[20]

Adults may also suffer from compulsive overeating, and such behavior is similarly unrelated to real hunger. For example, being fat can provide an excuse for failure in personal

Joel Pett for the Lexington Herald-Leader. Reprinted with permission.

relationships and at work. If a romance or career doesn't work out, they can blame their size, imagining that if they were thin, everything would be just fine. One psychiatrist specializing in obesity notes,

> Overeating has more to do with unconscious wishes and fears than anything else. . . . When an individual consistently or compulsively overeats, invariably that overeating is unconscious and symbolically represents something other than just eating. Incredulous as it may sound, although most overeaters desperately wish to be thin, on another level, an unconscious level, they wish to be fat and fear being thin.[21]

Researchers also find that the speed with which obesity in the United States has increased supports the view that environmental factors are to blame for obesity. In the ten years between the national health surveys, the rate of obesity increased from 24 to 33 percent. Ten years is much too short a time for a significant change to take place in the genetic makeup of the population, so nongenetic factors, these researchers argue, must be responsible.

Furthermore, scientists point out that regardless of their racial or ethnic heritage, Americans experience obesity at rates far higher than similar populations elsewhere in the world. As researcher Trevor Smith argues,

> Data show that Americans have the highest incidence of obesity in developed countries: for example obesity is twice as prevalent in the US as in France. . . . But the United States is a nation of immigrants. Do we really believe our current rate of obesity has become so much higher than for people in the countries of Europe, Asia and Africa from whom we descended, by genetic changes in so few generations? This does not seem reasonable. Besides, Asians who emigrate to the United States and change to American eating habits tend to become more overweight than those who stay at home. Weight gain does not wait for genetics, it crops up in a single generation and therefore is due mainly to diet, aided by less physical activity.[22]

The argument for heredity

Those who see obesity as inherited note that for millions of years the ability to store fat was an advantage for all animals, including humans:

Evolution perfected the fat storage mechanism of the human body. For millennia, periodic food shortages—as a result of drought, or catastrophe—were a way of life for our ancestors. Those people most likely to survive were those who during good times could convert extra food into body fat that served as insurance against the famine.[23]

The proponents of heredity as a cause of obesity argue that humans living today are likely to have inherited genes that encourage the body to eat well, store fat, and use calories most efficiently. Obesity, these experts contend, becomes a problem in modern industrialized nations like America, where famine is almost unheard of but the "fat genes" continue to operate.

Some experts believe that the human body evolved to store fat in case of famine.

Although evidence indicates that lack of exercise and overeating, regardless of their underlying causes, is directly responsible for the prevalence of obesity in the United States, many individuals, including some health professionals and researchers, continue to believe that heredity plays a role. In support of their argument, they point to studies of twins who, despite being separated at an early age and raised in different homes, show similar tendencies toward obesity.

Researchers who believe that environmental factors are to blame for obesity argue that studies of identical twins are flawed because they don't include records of what they ate. One researcher notes, "There are studies on identical twins that suggest that, when they are brought up in different environments, if one is obese it's probable that the other will be too. But in order to explain this only by heredity, you need long, detailed records of food choices and food intake. These data are unavailable."[24] In fact, because so little information is available on the contribution of many environmental factors to obesity, it is impossible to determine the extent of the genetic contribution to the condition.

Stable weight

Studies of twins who were raised apart yet grew up to have similar adult weights regardless of the environment in which they were raised are cited to support the theory that most people's adult weight is genetically predetermined at a particular set point, and that it is rare for individuals to stray from that weight by more than 10 percent. According to one doctor, who believes that obesity is a biological disease directly related to heredity, "Everybody has a weight that their body can defend. I think most people know what that weight is. You lose a little weight, but tend to bounce back to that same weight again and again and again."[25] Evidence that the body wants to maintain its set point is the fact that most people maintain a relatively stable weight over time in spite of great variations in the amount of food they eat and the amount of exercise they get. If body weight weren't set, the reasoning goes, then simply increasing the number of calories consumed by 150 per day would translate into a twenty-five-pound weight gain in one year. Proponents of the set-point theory claim that when a person tries to overpower the body's set point by dieting, the body responds by slowing down its metabolism so it can function on fewer calories. The set-point theory, its proponents argue, explains why so many weight-loss programs fail to keep a person's weight down for long.

Those who blame environmental or behavioral factors for obesity are unconvinced and point out that it's hard to separate genetic effects from learned habits. As one scientist explains, "Overweight parents who eat too much fat tend to

provide the same food choices for their children as for themselves, so their kids eat too much fat, too. This is not genetics; this is eating what is available."[26] Researchers note that a tendency toward obesity in a family is not necessarily a genetic predisposition because family members not only share common genes but also diet, cultural background, and many other aspects of lifestyle. Genes can predispose an individual to gaining weight, but whether he or she does depends a lot on environment, perhaps even before birth.

Studies show that children of obese parents are likely to become obese themselves.

Fetal programming

New research into what is called fetal programming is exploring the effects conditions in the womb have on adults. Researchers have suggested that many diseases, including obesity, may actually have their roots in the womb before birth. For example, some studies suggest that undernutrition on the part of the mother during the first three months of pregnancy is associated with obesity during adulthood. One doctor offers two possible explanations:

Some researchers believe obesity is linked to conditions of fetal experiences in the uterus during the first trimester.

If food is scarce during the first trimester, (the fetus's) metabolism is set so that every available calorie sticks. Or the availability or scarcity of food may affect the appetite centers in the fetal brain. In that case, undernutrition early in fetal life could dial up the appetite controls to the setting "eat whatever's around: you never know when famine will hit."[27]

When researchers reexamine twin studies in the context of fetal programming, their findings suggest that some traits that have been attributed to heredity, such as obesity, may instead reflect fetal programming since twins not only share the same genes but also the same environment in the womb.

Finding the middle ground

No single cause is associated with all cases of obesity. In all probability, obesity in the United States is a result of the interaction of genes with an environment that encourages a sedentary lifestyle and the consumption of too many calories. Although genes may make a person susceptible to obesity in a specific environment, obesity is not inevitable. Individuals with a genetic predisposition to obesity will still be thin if they live in an environment in which food is scarce or one that requires a lot of physical activity; individuals not genetically predisposed to obesity may still become fat in an environment that includes abundant, high-calorie foods and little physical activity.

As one writer summed it up, "Heredity strongly influences body size and shape but people don't inherit fatness the way they do eye color or skin tone. Instead, they may have a genetic predisposition toward obesity that makes them more vulnerable but not destined to be fat. To gain weight they still have to eat more calories than they burn."[28]

3

The Consequences of Obesity: More than Just a Health Issue

ALTHOUGH THE CAUSES of obesity are the subject of ongoing debate, there is little question of the consequences of obesity. In fact, obesity has been called one of the most pervasive health risks facing America today. Responsible for three hundred thousand deaths each year, obesity may well surpass smoking to become the greatest threat to Americans' well-being in the twenty-first century. As a disorder that affects more than one-third of all adults and one child out of five in America, obesity's consequences extend beyond physical health into the psychological, social, and economic well-being of the country.

The health consequences

A study completed in 1999 of more than 1 million Americans, the largest ever done on obesity and mortality, found that overweight people have a higher rate of premature death than people of normal weight do. Dr. JoAnn Mason, a specialist in preventive medicine, says, "The study settles once and for all any lingering questions about whether weight alone increases the risk of death and disease. The evidence is now compelling and irrefutable. Obesity is a very serious problem."[29] Obesity is associated with increases in illness and death from a variety of diseases. Of the many health problems that occur with greater frequency in obese people, the most important and common include high blood pressure, heart disease, diabetes, arthritis, and certain kinds of cancer. Studies show that even mild obesity (twenty to thirty pounds over ideal weight) heightens the risk of weight-related health problems. Moreover, the more overweight a person is, the greater the risk of dying from obesity-related diseases.

Although obese people as a group are more at risk of certain diseases, the level of risk varies among individuals. Obese adults are broadly divided into two categories depending on body shape and location of fat deposits. It's not clear why, but individuals with large fat deposits on their hips and thighs (pear shaped) are less susceptible to obesity-induced disease than are apple-shaped individuals, who store their fat in their abdominal area. Unlike fat on the hips and thighs, which just sits there and causes no harm, belly fat—called visceral abdominal fat—is active. For reasons that researchers still don't understand, visceral abdominal fat enters the bloodstream faster than hip fat and releases fatty acids into the vein that leads directly into the liver. These fatty acids interfere with the liver's job of breaking down insulin, which in turn disturbs the body's cholesterol equilibrium. Because of their tendency toward high levels of cholesterol, obese apple-shaped individuals have a significantly greater risk of heart disease, stroke, and diabetes.

Obesity and heart disease

Those who treat victims of heart disease identify obesity as a major cause of such problems. "I think excess weight is the worst coronary risk factor for men and women because it leads to unfavorable changes in blood fats, blood pressure and blood sugar, all of which increase the risk of heart attack,"[30] said one physician.

The ways in which obesity promotes heart disease are varied. For example, obesity contributes to congestive heart failure. When a person gains weight, the body manufactures more blood in order to carry oxygen and other nutrients to the new fat tissue. As a result, the heart has to work harder because it has to pump more blood. The left

Obesity is blamed for a variety of life-threatening problems, such as heart disease, high blood pressure, and diabetes.

ventricle, the heart chamber most responsible for pumping the blood out of the heart and pushing it through the thousands of blood vessels throughout the body, eventually becomes overdeveloped and enlarged. Finally, the enlarged ventricle fails and the heart stops—a classic coronary arrest.

Obesity also contributes to the most common form of heart disease in the United States, coronary artery disease. In this case, fatty plaques built up in the arteries cause a thickening of the artery wall and the consequent narrowing of the artery, which in turn deprives the heart of blood. When the heart is deprived of blood, it fails to receive sufficient oxygen and part of the heart muscle dies, causing a heart attack (also called a myocardial infarction). Other problems, however, while less dramatic, can be just as deadly in the long run.

Obesity and high blood pressure

An obese person's chances of developing high blood pressure are at least double what they are among people of normal weight. For a variety of reasons, the kidneys of obese individuals are less efficient at eliminating sodium from the body, leading to a buildup of this element in the blood. Because the body can only tolerate sodium in low concentrations, it needs water to dilute the sodium down to a safe level. The water the body retains to accomplish this task fills the arteries and veins with excess fluids, resulting in high blood pressure. The increased pressure strains the heart, creating the same conditions that lead to congestive heart failure. High blood pressure also damages the lining of the blood vessels themselves. In response to the damage, fatty deposits build up and the blood vessels narrow. Blockages may then develop, causing strokes and heart attacks.

Obesity and diabetes

In addition to increasing the risk of developing heart disease, obesity triples one's risk of developing diabetes. For reasons not completely understood, fat tissue increases the body's need for insulin. Again for reasons that are unclear, fat also creates a resistance to insulin, which makes obese

A nurse teaches a diabetic patient in a hospital how to inject himself with insulin. Obesity triples the risk of developing diabetes.

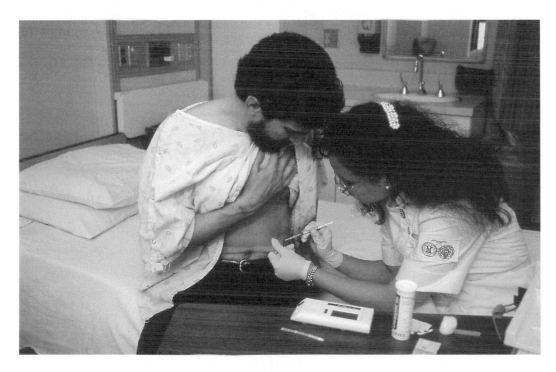

individuals prime candidates for the kind of diabetes known as type II diabetes mellitus, or adult onset diabetes. Experts believe that obesity accounts for the vast majority—more than 80 percent—of the cases of type II diabetes. Uncontrolled, diabetes can lead to major health problems, including heart disease, kidney failure, loss of vision, and amputation of limbs caused by poor circulation and infection.

Obesity and arthritis

Almost every bodily function is affected by obesity. In obese individuals the cartilage that serves as cushioning in a person's joints is subjected to excess wear and tear because of the excessive weight. Normally smooth cartilage then becomes rough and cracked and gradually loses its ability to cushion the joints. Osteoarthritis, the most common form of arthritis, results. According to the authors of *The PDR Family Guide to Nutrition and Health,* the problem is not confined to load-bearing joints:

> It makes sense that there's a link between osteoarthritis of the knees and being overweight: carrying an extra 50 pounds of baggage can wreak havoc on the knee joints. But recent research . . . found that people who were 20 percent or more overweight were also three times more likely than slimmer people to have osteoarthritis of the hands, and that their arthritis was more severe.[31]

Obesity and cancer

As if cardiovascular disease, diabetes, and arthritis weren't enough, studies show an especially clear association between excess weight and a higher risk of dying from a variety of cancers. Overweight men are more likely to die of colorectal and prostate cancer than are men of normal weight. Obese women have higher rates of cancer of the uterus, ovaries, and breasts. The processes by which obesity may contribute to development of cancers are complex and are not always completely understood by scientists. But the statistical links between obesity and these deadly diseases are clear enough to be alarming, given the large numbers of Americans who are at risk.

Although the role of obesity in the development of cancer is not completely understood, some researchers believe that obesity may somehow promote cancerous changes in cells. Because obese people have higher estrogen levels than people whose weight is normal, some researchers believe that cancer may be caused by the increased activity of this hormone.

It is clear that being overweight causes numerous complex biochemical disruptions in the human body. In recent years medical researchers have discovered links between obesity and an astonishing variety of other health problems. In addition to heart disease, diabetes, arthritis, and cancer, obesity has been linked with gallstones, back pain, sleep apnea (a condition characterized by brief periods when a person stops breathing while asleep), heartburn, gout, varicose veins, carpal tunnel syndrome, and immune system deficiencies. Studies also show that extremely obese women are almost twice as likely to experience difficulties in childbirth and have babies that suffer from serious birth defects.

Psychological problems caused by obesity

The consequences of obesity are not only physical. For example, obese children are particularly vulnerable to

Obesity-Induced Health Risks

arthritis	gout
back pain	heartburn
birth defects	heart disease
cancer	high blood pressure
carpal tunnel syndrome	immune deficiencies
diabetes	sleep apnea
gallstones	varicose veins

problems with social and psychological adjustment and self-esteem caused by being teased about their weight. Researcher Michael Loewy notes,

> Kids as young as five or six know that to call someone "fatso" is a way to hurt them. . . . In a 1995 study, researchers at Connecticut College showed silhouettes of thin, average and fat children to 30 first graders, asking which child was the "good" one and which one they'd most like to have as a friend. The majority said that the thin child was the good one and most wanted to be friends with the thin child.[32]

The teasing and isolation that overweight children endure is painful, to say the least. One overweight teen recalls, "All through my childhood I was taunted about my weight. Classmates would yell things like, 'Wide load!' or 'Cow!' or they would make mooing or oinking sounds as I passed. I wonder if they knew how much it hurt me."[33] Overweight youngsters may be stereotyped by teachers and other adults as lazy or lacking self-discipline. And the problems do not lessen as youngsters enter adolescence.

The psychological effects of obesity can be severe. Overweight children often face ridicule from peers.

One woman recalls the humiliation she endured as an obese teenager:

> The first time I ever undressed in the locker room, the other girls laughed and joked and pointed to the rolls and layers of blubber. . . . I never gave them another chance to hurt me like that. From that day on, I always wore my gym shorts and T-shirt under my clothes. My school clothes were a uniform, anyway: stretch pants and a knit top. What did it matter if I added another layer? Not many stylish clothes for teenagers come in size 46 and 48. There were no gym suits large enough to fit me, of course, and I never could wear a Girl Scout uniform. I was the only girl in my troop without one. I was also the only student in my high school hospital careers class without the traditional white coat. They didn't have one large enough.[34]

Ridiculed by their peers, deprived of places on sports teams and cheerleading squads, many fat students suffer from low self-esteem and appearance-related anxiety, which in turn increase the temptation to engage in other self-destructive behaviors. One study showed that overweight teens with poor self-image are most likely to take up smoking and drinking.

Social ostracism continues to dog overweight people into adulthood. Subtle put-downs and overt criticism erode their self-esteem. As one obese woman puts it,

> Being big means putting up with a lot of bigots, unwanted advice, crude comments and overall unfair treatment. Who among us hasn't had some insensitive person say something like: "you have such a pretty face but . . ." (Translation: you have the potential to be attractive and you blew it by getting so big) or "you know I'd go out with you IF you lost a few pounds" or "you aren't really going to wear that, are you? It doesn't compliment your shape" (Translation: you have far too many rolls [of fat] to wear anything that isn't extremely oversized and covers you from head to toe.) Then of course we have the people who are so tactless that they do things like buy you "slimfast" for your birthday (that's always fun) call you names, stare at you in restaurants.[35]

Overweight individuals are not only the butt of public scorn but also find that sometimes the world simply seems to ignore their needs. One woman who suffers from obesity sardonically describes the difficulty of finding fashionable clothing:

Perhaps I am too picky but, I tend to stay away from fashions that have not been in circulation for the past twenty or so years. I also admit that I shudder at the thought of wearing outfits that look like they should adorn the body of a circus clown. I am twenty one years of age, I want fashions that are found in the women's section but unfortunately I am stuck in the plus size department, which all too often consists of two or three racks of outdated garbage. I often see styles in the other department that I love and I know would look gorgeous on me, however, most of the people making the clothes today must feel that we large gals would prefer wearing a garment with all the charm of a burlap sack to that stunning crushed black velvet dress over there.[36]

Social and economic consequences

The problems faced by the obese go well beyond the world of fashion, however. Excess weight has financial consequences not only for obese individuals and their families but for the entire nation as well. Obesity-related health costs can be direct, in the form of doctor bills, or indirect, in the form of time missed from work. Together these costs exceed $68.8 billion every year. In addition, Americans spend more than $30 billion a year on weight-loss products and services.

Obese Americans personally experience enormous social and economic consequences. Although researchers disagree as to whether obesity contributes to poverty, there is little doubt that obese people suffer from some economic and social discrimination.

Such discrimination against fat people begins early. Studies have shown that obese high school graduates, for example, are less likely to be accepted at top colleges, even if they scored the same on achievement tests and had the same grades as their slimmer schoolmates. Once they graduate from college, overweight individuals have a harder time finding a job. Besides weight guidelines that organizations such as police and fire departments are legally entitled to enforce, potential employers often discriminate against obese job applicants. One woman recalled her experiences trying to get a job, saying that prospective employers often would be enthusiastic about her application but that attitudes often changed when she walked in for an interview: "All of a sudden [the interviewers] would get this look on their face. Then they'd give me a cursory interview and say, 'We're thinking of going with a more entry-level person' or 'We're rethinking our staffing needs.'"[37] Once they obtain a job, obese employees are less likely to get promoted.

Many employers are reluctant to hire obese individuals because they believe obesity leads to poor health, less energy on the job, and loss of productivity. Studies show that obesity affects organizations directly through higher health, life, and disability insurance rates and paid sick leave. In fact, obesity is estimated to account for 43 percent of all health care spending by American businesses.

Obese individuals face discrimination in the workplace, making it harder for them to find and keep good jobs.

Perhaps one reason that discrimination against the obese is still tolerated is the widely held belief that weight is something that a person can do something about. But as many people who have tried to lose weight or to help others to do so know, treating obesity is not just a simple matter of eating less.

4

Treating Obesity: Nothing Seems to Work

AT ANY GIVEN time in the United States 15 to 35 percent of Americans are trying to lose weight. Their goal is to achieve the American ideal—to be slim and fit. A $33-billion-dollar-a-year weight-loss industry promotes and markets thousands of treatments, devices, and programs that promise to help consumers lose weight and keep it off. Despite this enormous expenditure, the battle against obesity is difficult, continuous, and often futile.

Diets

An estimated 50 million Americans go on a diet of some kind every year. Unfortunately, the effort is often in vain. One victim of obesity writes,

> I've gained and lost over a thousand pounds in my life. I've been anorexic, sixty pounds overweight, and every point in between. I've been on the Atkins diet; the Prunes and Meatball Diet; the Thousand-Calorie-a-Day Sugar Diet; the Coffee, Diet Creme Soda and Cigarette Diet; Weight Watchers; and water fasts. All of them worked for a week, a month, even a year. And then every single one of them stopped working.[38]

Calorie-counting and weight-loss diets, which are commonplace today, were unknown until the end of the nineteenth century. Then, in 1863, an overweight English casket maker named William Banting published his *Letter on Corpulence,* explaining how he had lost weight. Banting had been so fat for most of his adult life that he had avoided going out in public because of the stares he attracted. After consulting many doctors about losing weight with no success, he finally met Dr. William Harvey, who put him on a starch-and-sugar-free diet. He lost a pound a week for thirty-five weeks. Banting's *Letter on Corpulence* sold more than fifty-eight thousand copies. It is considered the first modern book concerned with weight loss.

Five basic categories

Since 1900 more than twenty thousand diets have been published in books, magazines, and pamphlets. Despite their numbers, all diets can be placed in one of five basic categories: fixed-menu, exchange-type, formula, very low-calorie, and flexible diets. All of these diets have the common goal of helping the dieter correct the imbalance between caloric intake and use.

Fixed-menu diets provide lists of everything the dieter can eat for each meal. The advantage of this diet is that the food is preselected, eliminating questions of whether a particular food helps or hinders the goal of weight loss. One problem with such diets is that the food choices are limited, so the diet can get boring. A longer-term drawback of fixed-menu diets is that they fail to teach the dieter how to select nourishing and nonfattening foods to be eaten on a continuing basis.

One answer to the limitations of the fixed-menu diet is the exchange-type diet. Perhaps the best known of these is the Weight Watchers diet. The exchange type diet offers a meal plan with a set number of servings from each of several food groups. Foods within each group can then be interchanged as the dieter wishes. For example, in the starch category, the dieter can choose between one slice of bread or half a cup of oatmeal. The exchange-type diet offers the advantages of more day-to-day variety and therefore is easier to follow away from home. Although such diets teach food selection skills that are necessary to keep

weight off, many dieters find them too complicated to maintain for long periods of time.

Many dieters long for a simple, easy-to-prepare formula that will help them lose weight. Formula or liquid diets originated in Chicago in the 1930s with a product sold in beauty parlors called "Dr. Stoll's Diet-Aid, the Natural Reducing Food." Instructions recommended mixing the concoction of chocolate, starch, whole wheat, and bran with a cup of water and drinking it for breakfast and lunch. This approach to weight loss caught on, and in the late 1990s liquid diets like Slim-Fast and Nestlé Sweet Success crowd grocery store shelves. Convenient and easy to use, these nutritionally balanced blends of protein, carbohydrates, and fat consist of powder or liquid to be mixed with skim milk. Instructions advise dieters to consume these drinks in place of two daily meals and a snack.

Although people who use formula diets do lose weight, there are disadvantages. One nutritionist notes that, despite claims to the contrary, liquid diets still may not be complete:

A nutritionist counsels a patient about eating habits. Many Americans attempt to change their eating habits by dieting, but most results do not last.

The new generation of shakes is nutritionally balanced. However, as more is learned about the importance of phytochemicals—plant substances believed to protect against disease—there's just no way to know exactly how many of these nutrients you miss out on. Plus, liquid dieting doesn't instill the healthy eating habits that you need to maintain healthy weight loss once you go off the shakes.[39]

Since the 1930s, various formula diets have been developed. Such products are often ineffectual and sometimes harmful in the long run.

Most users lose weight quickly on the formula diet, but unless they implement long-term behavioral changes, they gain it back as soon as they stop using the formula.

Some diets are simply so restrictive that they are only appropriate for people most severely afflicted with obesity. Very-low-calorie diets (VLCDs) are commercially prepared formulas of eight hundred calories or less that are consumed in place of all other food. VLCDs are supposed to be used only under a doctor's supervision and are generally recommended only for severely to morbidly obese people (those with a BMI greater than thirty). Although dieters lose a lot of weight in a short time (about three to five pounds a week), VLCDs are no more effective than other diets when it comes to maintaining the new, lower weight. Moreover, many dieters on VLCDs suffer minor physical side effects like fatigue, constipation, nausea, and diarrhea, although these usually subside after a while. One more serious complication that some users of these diets experience is the formation of gallstones. Researchers are uncertain whether the gallstones are caused by the

VLCDs themselves or are somehow a side effect of the weight loss.

If the goal is to help a dieter adopt new behavior patterns, a diet that maximizes food choices would seem to be an answer. Flexible diets provide this choice, monitoring fat only, calories only, or a combination of the two with the dieter choosing the type and amount of food consumed. While some flexible diets do provide the opportunity for people to learn how to control what they eat, many diets fail to address the issue of nutritional balance. For example, a diet that only controls the amount of fat consumed may let the dieter consume unlimited calories from sugar and therefore fail to result in weight loss.

Fad and crash diets

Of the millions of American dieters, many choose sensible low-calorie, low-fat diets. But others in search of a magic solution to their obesity turn to fad or crash diets. Since the 1920s thousands of fad diets have been promoted that promise easy weight loss if a person eats a certain food or combination of foods. Fad diets usually focus on one food, not necessarily associated with dieting, and claim that that particular food has previously unrecognized weight-loss properties.

Fad diets seem simple and most even work in the short term. But they rarely have any permanent effect because most fad diets, although they may sound scientifically sophisticated, simply come down to radically reducing calories. After the initial weight loss, once dieters go back to normal eating, they quickly regain the weight they have lost, and often more. And many find it even harder to lose that weight the next time they go on a diet.

Another problem with fad or crash diets is that they are usually not well-balanced. Such regimens can cause nutritional deficiencies and serious health problems if followed for a long time because any diet based on a single food cannot provide all of the nutrients the human body needs to stay healthy.

People often measure the success of a diet by the numbers they read on a scale, rather than by its nutritional attributes.

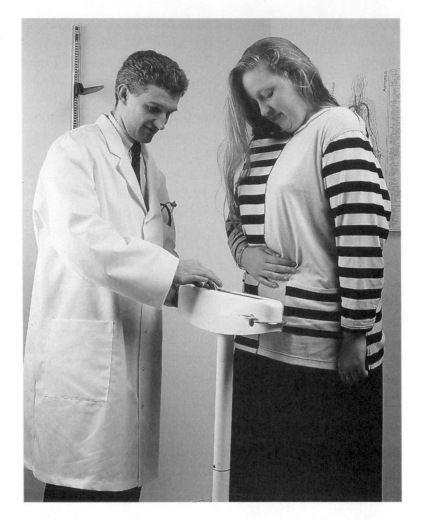

Other fad diets emphasize loading up on one food group to the exclusion of another, requiring, for instance, large quantities of protein and restricting carbohydrates like bread, pasta, grains, potatoes, and sugar. Although initial weight loss on such a diet is high, there are serious consequences. Along with the protein they require, these diets are full of fat and cholesterol, which is bad for the heart. Individuals who faithfully follow these diets can fail to get all of the vitamins and minerals required for good health. High-protein diets can result in the depletion of the body's store of carbohydrates, with consequences ranging from bad breath to headaches, dizziness, fatigue, and nausea.

Too much protein also overworks the kidneys, which can eventually cause serious, irreparable damage to these vital organs.

The yo-yo effect

Although many dieters experience initial success, fewer than 1 percent of all dieters who manage to lose weight are able to keep it off. Worse, 30 percent of dieters regain all of the weight they lost, and more besides. Some researchers, referring to this phenomenon as the yo-yo effect, go so far as to claim that dieting may be the major cause of obesity. They believe that diets are destined to fail because the human body

Many fad diets involve the consumption of only a certain kind of food. Diets of this sort, like the all-protein diet, have negative side effects.

evolved to prevent weight loss and will fight to regain any weight that has been lost. Proponents of the yo-yo theory believe that weight loss causes the metabolism to slow down because the body sees the drop in calories as a threat of famine.

Other scientists are unwilling to go quite so far as to blame obesity on dieting. Dr. F. Xavier Pi-Sunyer, one of the country's leading experts in obesity, notes that concern about the yo-yo effect may be overblown: "There is no convincing data for the claim that yo-yoing makes you fatter but it has somehow gotten into the media in a large way, so people have gotten confused about whether they are actually harming themselves by trying to lose weight."[40] The fact is that although metabolism drops when weight is lost, when the weight is regained and the body no longer perceives the threat of famine, the metabolism rebounds.

Modifying behavior

Since dieting alone is so ineffective in the long run, some weight-loss experts advocate a combination of diet and behavioral modification offered by various commercial weight-loss programs. These commercial programs have proven enormously popular. According to a *Consumer Reports* survey, 20 percent of the people trying to lose weight use commercial weight-loss programs. Some clinics provide frozen, canned, or packaged food or other supplements that must be purchased from the clinic. Others sell packaged meals to their clients and offer group exercise classes as well. Weight Watchers, one of the oldest and most successful of the commercial programs, offers peer support with an exchange diet using prepackaged food that can be purchased at the supermarket.

Weight-loss clinics promote various methods for losing weight, but all promise that the individual dieter will receive expert or professional support—for a price. Data about the effectiveness of commercial centers are scarce, but available studies indicate that although individuals lose weight while participating in the programs, they tend to regain the weight after completing them.

Getting at the root of the problem

Not every weight-loss program works by treating obesity directly. A number of weight-loss programs try to help dieters deal with the underlying causes of overeating. Take Off Pounds Sensibly (TOPS), a nonprofit, noncommercial weight-loss group, was started in 1948 by a homemaker in Milwaukee, Wisconsin. TOPS works in tandem with each member's personal physician and provides support, encouragement, and nutritional education to its members through weekly group meetings. After a confidential weigh-in, each meeting features a presentation by a physician, nutritionist, psychologist, or other health professional. Members follow whatever diet and exercise program is prescribed by their own doctor; the meetings are a place for members to share their weight-loss successes and challenges and to offer each other suggestions and support. TOPS has 275,000 members in 11,000 chapters in the United States and Canada.

Other weight-loss programs take their cue from successful efforts to treat people for addictive disorders like alcoholism. Overeaters Anonymous (OA) was founded in 1960 by several people who had tried everything to lose weight and had failed. Inspired by the success of Alcoholics Anonymous (AA), the group adopted the principles of AA's Twelve Step Program, which is based on abstinence. OA has no dues or membership fees, it is not a diet club, and it makes no promises of weight loss:

> By admitting inability to control compulsive overeating in the past, and abandoning the idea that all one needs to be able to eat normally is "a little willpower," it becomes possible to abstain from overeating—one day at a time. OA offers members support in dealing with the physical and emotional symptoms of compulsive overeating and recommends emotional, spiritual and physical recovery changes through the Twelve Steps.[41]

OA members are encouraged to consult a health professional for their individual diet. Today there are approximately eighty-five hundred OA groups in over fifty countries throughout the world.

5

Products and Procedures to Treat Obesity

Despite all of the efforts by researchers and all of the hard work on the part of dieters, the vast majority of obese Americans find themselves unable to lose weight and keep it off. The temptation, therefore, is to try other measures, some of which are of only questionable safety and effectiveness.

Appetite suppressants

Since the direct cause of obesity is the taking in of more calories than are used, it is natural to conclude that reducing a person's appetite should help control weight. Faced with repeated diet failures, many overweight Americans dream of losing weight quickly and painlessly through the use of medications and other products. Although science has yet to come up with the miraculous cure for obesity, many overweight people pin their hopes on one of the drugs designed to suppress appetite. The effectiveness of most of these drugs is questionable, and some of them are actually dangerous.

Prescription diet drugs to help control the appetite have been available since the 1960s. The earliest prescription appetite suppressants were amphetamines. Amphetamines have unpleasant side effects, however, including insomnia and irritability. Other side effects are even more serious, including strokes, heart attacks, and acute depression. They are also highly addictive. Moreover, when users stop taking amphetamines, their appetite increases dramatically and they regain all of the weight they have lost and more.

By the mid-1990s, far more sophisticated medications were available to help people control their appetites. When the Food and Drug Administration (FDA) approved the use of two prescription diet compounds in the 1990s, prescription drug therapy for obesity suddenly became big business. The two medications, dexfenfluramine (sold as Redux) and fenfluramine and phentermine (known as Fen-Phen), were called miracle drugs and heralded by the press as saviors for people who hadn't been able to lose weight in the past.

Seemingly overnight, a number of physicians established diet-pill clinics and attracted patients into their offices with advertisements exclaiming medical breakthroughs that promised quick, safe, and permanent results. Some commercial weight-loss programs also entered into the medical prescription market by hiring doctors who could prescribe diet drugs at the program center. Many doctors, however,

Frustrated by dieting failures, some people turn to appetite-suppressing drugs like Redux to help them lose weight.

saw problems looming. One physician observed that Americans' obsession with being thin leads them to take risks they would never take otherwise:

> If overweight/obesity were like any other disease, such as diabetes or hypertension physicians would prescribe a medication only to their own patients, taking into account the potential risks and benefits as they pertain to that specific individual. Moreover, the patient would be reluctant to take a prescription from another clinician, one who may not be aware of his/her personal background and medical problems. If this were the case, diet drug usage would be well controlled and monitored. But obesity is not like any other disease. The drive to thinness is fueling a $33 billion weight loss industry. Out of desperation, the public turns to any and all quick-fix weight reduction promotions.
>
> When properly prescribed and used, appetite suppressant medications can be an extremely beneficial adjunct in the treatment of patients with obesity. On the other hand, these same medications have been shown to be a convenient and highly profitable product for entrepreneurs wishing to cash in on a vulnerable group of consumers. The most disturbing aspect of this unintended use of medications is that individuals who should not have been prescribed drugs in the first place, may have been harmed.[42]

The problems with the new diet drugs soon came to light. In 1996 primary pulmonary hypertension, a rare cardiopulmonary disease in which the blood vessels in the lungs constrict and narrow, leading to heart failure, was linked to the use of dexfenfluramine. Then, in 1997, Fen-Phen was found to be associated with the development of leaky heart valves. The FDA asked the drug manufacturers to voluntarily withdraw the drugs from the market, and they did. Although Fen-Phen is no longer on the market, some doctors prescribe Phen-Pro, which is a combination of phentermine and the antidepressant medicine Prozac.

Undeterred by such failures, researchers continue the hunt for safe and effective appetite suppressants. Another medication, sibutramine, sold under the brand name Meridia, was made available in 1997. The drug works on chemicals produced in the brain to reduce appetite and make people feel full. Meridia helps some users, particu-

larly on the first six months of a diet, but it doesn't work at all for others. The drug's main drawback is that it may increase blood pressure and heart rates in some patients, leaving its safety open to question.

Fat blockers

With so few positive results and so many problems caused by appetite suppressants, dieters have turned their hopes to a new kind of magic pill—one that allows them to eat whatever and as much as they want without gaining weight. As one obesity specialist says, "The holy grail of diet drugs is simple in conception—a pill that stops the body from absorbing calories from food after it's been eaten, not just supplementing willpower, but making willpower unnecessary."[43] In 1999 the FDA approved Orlistat, the first drug that controls weight by interfering with the body's absorption of fat. The drug works in the intestinal tract by blocking the action of lipase, a digestive enzyme that breaks down fat. Instead of going into the bloodstream, 30 percent of the fat consumed in a meal accumulates in the intestines and is excreted in the feces.

Orlistat is not the magic pill that allows a dieter to eat unlimited quantities of fat without consequences, though. Unfortunately, by blocking the absorption of fat, the drug also blocks absorption of beta-carotene and the fat-soluble vitamins A, D, E, and K, so patients must take daily vitamin supplements in order to get these vital nutrients. Moreover, a person who eats more than twenty grams of fat in a meal (about the equivalent of two tablespoons of mayonnaise) is liable to experience side effects including bloating, cramps, flatulence, and diarrhea. In fact, the side effects are unpleasant enough that the drug's real benefit may be not as a fat blocker but as providing an incentive for not eating too much fat in the first place.

Non-prescription diet drugs are now available in many supermarkets and drug stores. However, these drugs also have many unwanted side effects.

Although many reputable physicians are reluctant to prescribe medications for weight loss, many nonprescription diet pills that work the same way as prescription drugs are available over the counter in drug stores and supermarkets. The FDA allows only two drugs to be used in nonprescription diet pills. The appetite suppressant phenylpropanolamine (PPA), which is chemically related to amphetamines, is sold under many different names: Acutrim, Control, Dexatrim, Hunger-Plus, and many more. Although these products are considered safe and effective when used as directed, they are not safe for everyone and may cause serious health problems if the recommended dose is exceeded. Furthermore, as with many other treatments, these medications do not help the obese person who wants to overcome the underlying cause of his or her condition.

An attractive target for charlatans

In addition to FDA-approved over-the-counter diet aids, hundreds of weight-loss products are available through the mail and in health-food stores. Desperate to lose weight and frustrated by repeated failures to do so, some victims of obesity are victimized a second time by hucksters who promise far more than they can deliver. One such product, starch blockers, usually sold in pill form, is claimed by their manufacturers to block the digestion of starches so a person could eat up to six hundred calories a day of starches like bread, potatoes, and pasta and not gain weight. No valid scientific studies have proven this product to be effective, however. Not only do starch blockers not work, but they can cause nausea, vomiting, diarrhea, and stomach pains. "Bulk producers," or "fillers," claim to promote weight loss by causing a full feeling in the stomach. Promoters claim that when bulk producers are taken before meals, they absorb liquids and swell in the stomach to form a gel and reduce hunger. Most fillers are ineffective but harmless. Some, however, can cause obstructions in the intestines, stomach, or esophagus.

Weight loss products and devices

Still other overweight Americans turn to gadgets, devices, and lotions in hopes of winning the battle against obesity. "Burn fat while you sleep" and "Lose ugly inches off your waist instantly" are just a few of the hundreds of claims made by promoters of weight-loss products, most of which are ineffective.

Although most gadgets that are promoted as weight-loss aids are harmless, other weight-loss devices may contribute to serious health problems. Body wraps, a popular type of reducing device, claim to dissolve fat deposits. Composed of bands of rubber or plastic worn around the hips, waists, thighs, or entire body, body wraps are claimed by promoters to be effective if worn while exercising, sleeping, or going about one's daily business. The only weight loss such devices cause, however, is attributable only to dehydration. Lost weight reappears as soon as the fluid is replaced. Worse, the dehydration that wraps cause can be harmful and even deadly.

When extreme measures are necessary

For patients who are exceedingly obese, doctors sometimes recommend more drastic treatments. For example, an individual's jaws can be wired together, making it impossible to open the mouth to eat. While the jaws are wired shut (usually six to twelve weeks), the patient drinks liquids through a straw. Although individuals may lose a great deal of weight, most of it is gained back when the wires are removed and they begin eating solid food again. Besides being uncomfortable, jaw wiring can cause infection and tooth decay because the teeth cannot be cleaned properly.

For the most extreme cases of obesity, physicians may prescribe the most drastic treatment of all, weight-loss surgery. The surgical procedure most commonly used today limits the amount of food the stomach can hold by closing off parts of the stomach. In this operation, popularly known as stomach stapling, the doctor closes off most of the stomach to create a "ministomach," which fills with food faster so the patient feels full sooner and eats less. After the surgery patients can only eat small amounts of food at a time, and food must be chewed very thoroughly, which helps the patient feel satisfied. Although most patients do lose weight, the operation can have serious complications, including infection from leakage, diarrhea, vomiting, intestinal blockage, gallstones, and malnutrition. The consequences of such side effects can even be deadly. Some people who undergo the surgery decide that the results do not justify the problems.

One woman who ultimately had her bypass surgery reversed describes her experience:

> I was told I would die if I didn't lose weight. I was also informed that there was now a way to lose weight which didn't require willpower. It was a surgical procedure called the intestinal bypass. Out of everything the doctor said, I heard only "You can eat and still lose weight" and "You will have a lot of diarrhea."

> I waited until my weight reached 308 pounds and then submitted to the operation. Thus began eight years of hell. The lowest point my weight reached after the bypass was 240 pounds. Then it began to yo-yo. I had diarrhea so badly I could not leave the house for a whole year. I finally got so I could control this condition somewhat, and then the flatulence started. It was very degrading. After three years, I started having kidney trouble. That was the beginning of a five-year ordeal during which I had twenty-five operations, eleven related to the damaged kidney.[44]

Despite the serious drawbacks, some experts point out that surgical treatment may have a profound and positive impact on the health and state of mind of some clinically obese individuals. One study of patients who had undergone the surgery showed that although they still remained overweight, they showed improvements in physical activity, general mental health, vitality, and social function. Patricia Choban, a surgeon who specializes in this operation, explains: "Simply removing some of the burden seems to be enough to make a big change in their daily lives. For many of them the success of losing some of their weight proves that they're not bad people who can never change. And that makes a big difference in their self-images."[45]

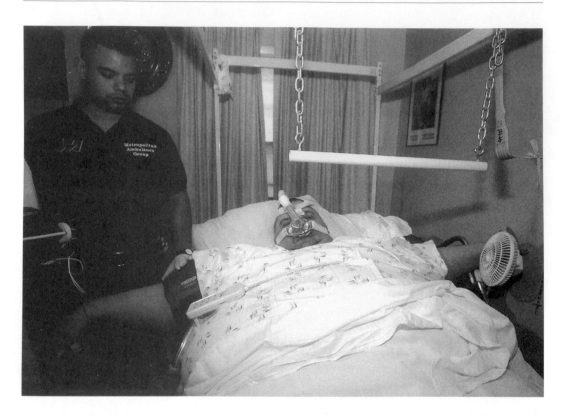

Morbidly obese people often take drastic measures such as weight-loss surgery. These surgeries have many long term health risks.

In spite of the fact that weight-loss surgery is only recommended for morbidly obese patients (people who are more than 100 percent over their desirable weight), at least some surgeons who specialize in the procedure aggressively market their services and claim that the surgery (which can cost upwards of twenty thousand dollars) is appropriate for anyone who is one hundred or more pounds overweight. However, these surgical procedures are major operations with short- and long-term complications, and patients need to understand the risks and the need for lifelong medical supervision after surgery.

A healthy attitude

Faced with the failure of almost every known treatment for obesity, many health professionals urge a reexamination of attitudes about obesity, pointing out that health, not appearance, should be the focus. "Much of the motivation for dieting is based upon a dissatisfaction with appearance that cannot be fixed by dieting. For most people, no amount of weight loss will transform their bodies to look like models or movie stars," says one health professional. "Too much emphasis is placed on weight loss and not enough is placed on improving health and well-being."[46]

In addition, realistic goals are critical for success. People who start out with unrealistic notions about how much weight they can lose or keep off over time may just give up when they experience repeated failures. Many overweight individuals could benefit from losing as little as five to ten percent of their weight and keeping it off—a goal that seems far more realistic than attempting to reach some arbitrary "ideal" size and weight.

Writer Geneen Roth notes that those who want to look like models may well be pursuing a phantom:

> When I look at the bodies of normal women, I am reminded that no one looks like the pictures we see in the magazines. Even the models don't look like the pictures we see of them.

Photographs are often retouched to erase a few inches from the legs and arms and remove any cellulite, sags, droops or imperfections that make a body human. Normal women have wrinkles, sags and cellulite. But since we don't compare ourselves to normal women, we end up feeling as if our bodies are wrong.[47]

Many health professionals now agree on the need to change the definition of success. As one doctor explains,

A sea change has occurred in the scientific thinking about weight loss—from reaching "ideal weight" to a modest five to fifteen percent reduction in weight. Modest weight reduction improves other health conditions. The typical patient can lose ten to fifteen percent of total weight and that is success, not failure. We have to help people modify their expectations about success. The message is that therapeutic weight loss is a success. The message is that there are significant health benefits of modest weight reduction and increased physical activity. We need to change the definition of success.[48]

The fat-acceptance movement

Despite the billions of dollars spent on diet products, many Americans are still overweight. However, instead of continuing what they see as the futile battle to reduce their bodies to fit the American ideal of slenderness, some overweight Americans have decided to accept their bodies the way they are. In the early 1970s a group of women who had dieted all of their lives without success formed what they called the Fat Underground and wrote the *Fat Manifesto,* which denounced America's cult of thinness. The women wrote articles for magazines and newspapers about the myths of dieting. They also worked to overcome discrimination against obese people by becoming active in the National Association to Advance Fat Acceptance (NAAFA). Once a social group for fat people, the organization was transformed by the women of the Fat Underground into an activist organization that works to protect the civil rights of obese Americans.

In addition to working to gain legal protection for fat people in the workplace, NAAFA's activists fight offensive and negative images of fat people in the mass media. Similarly, NAAFA's Kids Project helps children deal with their

anxieties related to weight and body image and promotes healthy eating and exercise by providing speakers and curriculum materials to schools. The Kids Project works to combat weight-related teasing and boost self-esteem among children of all sizes. NAAFA also works with obesity researchers in an effort to shift the emphasis of research away from finding ways to make fat people thin to ways to make fat people healthy. Likewise, the organization encourages members to make sensible food choices, follow an exercise program, and get regular medical checkups.

Marilyn Wan, a leading spokesperson for the fat-acceptance movement, says,

> People need to reacquaint themselves with their body, to normalize their attitude toward food, to find out when they are hungry and when they are full. Food must become a nonissue; nothing is off limits. They need to redefine exercise as something they do because it feels good, not because it is good for them. They need to break the connection between healthy habits of eating well and exercising to any expectation about

Some Americans fight the fat battle, not by losing weight, but by promoting the acceptance of individuals, regardless of weight.

weight loss. They need to move away from concerns about looks to concerns about health. It is important to do things they enjoy, form good habits for a lifetime, not diet or exercise because they are expecting to lose weight. When they normalize their attitude toward food, they will find out when they are hungry and when they are full. Expecting to lose weight sets a person up for failure. Because—when they try to lose weight—any improvements they make on a diet or exercise program are temporary and stop when the weight is lost. The healthy approach is to refuse to focus on weight. Focus on health.[49]

6

Preventing Obesity

"THE PROBLEM WITH obesity is once you have it it's very difficult to treat. What you want to do is prevent it,"[50] says Dr. F. Xavier Pi-Sunyer, a leading expert in obesity. If diets don't work, drugs are dangerous, and surgery and scams are unacceptable, the question of how to solve America's obesity problem remains. More and more experts are reaching agreement that the solution rests in preventing obesity by establishing healthy eating and exercise habits among Americans.

Preventing childhood obesity

Research indicates that habits that contribute to obesity are established early. Simply put, fat children grow up to be fat adults. According to one expert,

> Parents can spare their children a lifetime of weight woes by helping them keep lean, especially during their preteen growth spurt when fat cells multiply. The scary thing is if children have an excess of fat cells as preteens, they're 80 percent more likely to be obese as adults. The more fat cells you have, the more body fat you'll have because that's the way fat cells are preprogrammed. So prevention is the key.[51]

Parents are in a position to instill in their children healthy habits that prevent obesity. Because they are responsible for providing the food in the home—especially when children are very young—they can determine what kinds of food will be available for their youngsters to eat. If the kitchen is full of snacks like potato chips, cakes, cookies, and ice cream, the children will eat these high-calorie, high-fat foods. If, on the other hand, the refrigerator is stocked with fresh vegetables cut up into bite-sized pieces, fruit, and nonfat yogurt and the cupboards are stocked with pretzels, popcorn, and low-fat crackers, children will be more likely to snack on these low-calorie, low-fat treats. One writer who battled obesity recalls how her upbringing encouraged poor eating habits:

> We seldom had fresh fruit in the house, yet somehow we always had the money for candy, pastries, or ice cream. . . . Mom always packed an abundance of sweets and goodies for any trip. She baked cookies by the dozens. She baked her famous applesauce cake for every trip. . . . Mom and Dad would buy volumes of bread, fruit pies, bear claws and other pastries. The bread went swiftly into the freezer while the fruit pies, bear claws and pastries went swiftly into our mouths. We ate them right out of the grocery bags. Before dinner.[52]

Parents also can help their children by monitoring what they drink. Juice, long considered a healthy alternative to soft drinks, is a significant factor in childhood weight gain. Children may drink five hundred to a thousand calories a day in juice alone. One study showed that preschoolers who drank a cup and a half of juice or more per day were nearly two times as likely to have a weight problem as those who drank less. For a toddler, consumption of three hundred calories more a day than are burned off will cause a weight gain of five extra pounds a year.

Healthy eating also involves appropriate times and locations for eating. Experts recommend that parents also establish rules about eating such as regular (but not rigid) times when children are expected to sit at the table and eat dinner with the rest of the family. Most of these experts recommend not permitting youngsters to eat in front of the television or at the computer.

Another way parents can teach healthy eating is by helping children to monitor their own eating. Experts say they should not force children to clean their plates or to eat when they are not hungry just because it's meal time. If children don't learn to listen to their bodies, to eat when they're hungry and to stop when they're full, even if there is food on their plate, they may end up as obese adults.

Eating habits form early in a person's life, making it crucial that parents promote healthy eating and monitor their child's food intake.

In addition to teaching their children to monitor their eating, adults can foster a healthy attitude toward the role of food in children's lives. Youngsters, experts advise, should be encouraged to taste each new food, but they should never be forced to eat foods they hate. Children, these experts say, should be taught that food is for fuel and that eating is not a helpful response when they are mad, bored, or sad.

Many people eat almost unconsciously, often in combination with other activities such as watching television.

Establishing healthy eating habits

Making wise food choices is key to preventing obesity and maintaining a healthy weight, but it is also important to establish healthy eating habits. People eat (and overeat) for many reasons that have nothing to do with hunger. Many people eat almost unconsciously, even when they are not hungry, and hardly notice what they are eating. One writer cites habit as a cause for overeating:

> You're not hungry, you don't necessarily like the food. You don't even realize what you're doing—but you continuously shovel it in. . . . As we clear the breakfast dishes, we unconsciously clear all leftovers, all scraps, all spills—not into the garbage—but, gasp, into our mouths. As we make lunch for our little ones, without thinking about it, we pop a whole peanut-butter-and-jelly sandwich into our mouths, one tiny quarter at a time. As we clean up after lunch, we, again, simulate a human garbage can; before we put the lid on the peanut butter, we dip the knife in one more time. Ditto for the jam. "Oops, a few chips fell out of the bag," and "Why bother putting the last of the milk away?" . . . Most of this nibbling is done without thinking, simply because the food is there.[53]

Americans are so used to eating because they're either bored, sad, happy, or simply distracted by watching television or reading that they may have lost track of the actual need for food. The most important thing they have to learn is to listen to their body and eat when they feel hungry and stop when they feel full.

One way to establish healthy eating habits is to make time for meals rather than eat on the run. Geneen Roth, who has researched the subject of obesity, notes that people often do not concentrate on what they are doing when they eat. "Every day, in every moment, we spend our lives thinking about what we already did or are going to do, and we completely miss what we are doing. It's like eating a fabulous meal while talking on the phone or watching television. The meal ends and you didn't taste a thing because your attention was somewhere else."[54]

Where and when people eat can be as important as what they eat. Setting specific meal times and taking the time to sit down at a dinner table helps people avoid snacking.

Many obesity experts recommend that people follow a few simple rules to keep track of their eating. They stress the

importance of setting a place and sitting at the table to eat. "Sitting down allows you to concentrate and take pleasure from what you are doing. It also dispels the notion that you are not really eating while you are standing."[55] Experts also advise people never to eat between meals; instead, they should eat frequent low-calorie meals so that they are not hungry and tempted to snack. It is best to eat with a knife, fork, and spoon, and never swallow a mouthful of food without pausing to chew it slowly and thoroughly. Skipping a meal is to be avoided because that sometimes leads to overeating later. Planning menus and keeping healthy foods on hand also helps to avoid splurges on fat- or sugar-laden foods.

What to eat

Scientists have determined that, in general, the healthiest diet for everyone is one that is low in fat and high in complex carbohydrates and fiber. To make it easier to understand what this means in terms of real food, researchers at the U.S. Department of Agriculture (USDA) created the Food Guide Pyramid, a pictorial representation of the government's official nutritional recommendations for a healthy diet. The pyramid is divided into four levels of decreasing size: level one contains the bread, cereal, rice, and pasta group; level two contains the vegetable and fruit groups; the dairy and protein groups are on level three; and the group containing fats, oils, and sweets is on level four. The base of the pyramid, the largest part, pictures the food group from which people should eat the most. The levels get smaller going up the pyramid, indicating that people should eat fewer servings of the foods on the higher levels.

The pyramid also shows the amount of food that one should eat from each category, defined by the number of recommended servings per day. Because it is difficult for most people to define a serving, all packaged, canned, and frozen foods are required to indicate the measurement of a serving on the label. A serving of bread, for example, is one slice; a serving of milk is one cup, or eight ounces.

Various levels

According to the scientists who designed the food pyramid, people should get the greatest percentage of calories in their total diet from the first level of the pyramid—the bread, cereal, rice, and pasta group. These foods contribute carbohydrates, fiber, and B vitamins, and they are, for the most part, low in fat. The second level, which is divided into two kinds of food—vegetables and fruits—provides many nutrients that are essential to staying healthy, including vitamins A and C and folic acid. By themselves, fruits and vegetables tend to be very low in calories. The foods in the third group, dairy products, are excellent sources of protein and calcium—the nutrients responsible for building strong bones and teeth and creating new tissue. Dairy foods can range from no-fat (as in skim milk, nonfat yogurt, and nonfat cottage cheese) to high-fat content (such as ice cream, which can be as much as 70 percent fat). The trick is to get the greatest amount of calcium while minimizing consumption of fat.

Also on level three is the food group containing meat, poultry, fish, dry beans, eggs, and nuts, which are rich sources of protein and iron. These foods provide many of the raw materials for building new cells and are essential. Like the dairy group, the fat content varies significantly among particular foods. Beans and other legumes, for example, have the least fat while nuts have the most. Researchers now believe that a person does not need to get more than 15 percent of his or her total calories from this group.

Level four, at the tip of the pyramid (the smallest part), is the fats, oils, and sweets group, which consists of foods and cooking ingredients like oil, butter, mayonnaise, margarine, cream cheese, bacon, olives, whipping cream, candy, and soda. Since foods in this group contain few or no essential nutrients, they are often called "empty-calorie" foods. For a healthy diet, no more than 30 percent of the calories should come from fat. So, although experts say that no foods should be forbidden, higher-fat foods should be eaten in smaller amounts and less often.

The food pyramid was designed to help people develop healthy, balanced diets.

Establishing the food pyramid is regarded as a positive step toward teaching eating habits that will prevent obesity, but some experts think that the U.S. government should take even stronger measures. In 1998 Dr. Kelly Brownell, director of the Center for Eating and Weight Disorders at Yale University, proposed a tax on fatty foods (dubbed "the Twinkie tax") that would make them more expensive, pricing them out of the reach of many children and their parents. He also thinks the government should ban junk food advertising and eliminate soft drinks and fast food from schools. "A Twinkie tax might sound outlandish now," Brownell says, "but 30 years ago the idea of cigarette advertising bans, ordinances on public smoking, heavy taxes and lawsuits against tobacco companies were bold or unheard of ideas."[56]

Exercise

Teaching healthy eating habits is one strategy for preventing obesity, but exercise is also a crucial element in preventing (as well as treating) obesity. One doctor observes,

> Encouraging lifelong, regular exercise in children may well
> have the greatest effect in terms of preventing obesity, as well
> as numerous other benefits. If the time children now spend in
> front of the television eating junk food and watching adver-
> tisements for more junk food was instead spent in physical
> activity, leanness would be virtually ensured.[57]

Playing outside with friends, riding bicycles, and playing soccer, basketball, or baseball are important to everyday health. Parents who not only encourage their children to participate in these activities but also set an example by being active themselves help their kids to establish healthy habits that will serve to keep them healthy.

In their joint initiative Shape Up America! campaign, former U.S. surgeon general, Dr. C. Everett Koop and the National Association for Sport and Physical Education (NASPE) promote the idea that the solution for parents seeking to prevent obesity in their children begins with the parents' commitment to spend time being active with their kids. As Dr. Koop explains,

> When we talk about family values, we seem to overlook the
> importance of physical activity as a healthy way that the fam-
> ily can spend time together. Unless parents recognize that
> physical activity is important for the health of the whole fam-
> ily, everyone will pay the price in terms of obesity and an in-
> creased risk of disability and disease.[58]

Family activities can be as simple as taking the family's pet for a walk, running, jogging, or playing sports together.

The Shape Up America! campaign also stresses the importance of parents becoming advocates of daily school physical education at all grade levels. According to Judith Young, executive director of NASPE, "Parents are the key ingredient in making sure that schools provide appropriate experiences for children to develop physical fitness and physical competence. As a result, parents need to take as much interest in a child's physical education activities as in their academic course work."[59] On their part, physical education teachers and coaches should be encouraged to develop new attitudes toward exercise and athletics. According to former U.S. surgeon general Dr. C. Everett Koop, physical education classes should no

Teaching youngsters the benefits of exercise, like bicycle riding, will help them develop habits that will keep them healthy throughout their lives.

longer be considered training camps for athletes but rather a place to instill habits that will make students active for the rest of their lives. Teaching children how to be active for life is more important than teaching them skills for specific sports like basketball or football.

Many experts agree that the key to preventing obesity is to stop the trend among Americans toward ever more sedentary lives. Exercise is crucial in helping one to maintain a healthy weight. Approximately 75 percent of the calories a person consumes go to maintain normal body functions, but the other 25 percent are up for grabs. These calories can be used up in physical activity (exercise) or can pile up on the body as fat. Exercise not only burns off calories but also increases muscle tissue, which, even at rest, burns more calories than fat does.

Kinds of exercise

Researchers trying to determine what kind and how much exercise is best have come up with various recommendations. Some researchers contend that vigorous aerobic exercise three times a week is best, others recommend thirty minutes a day of moderate exercise, still others prefer walking or lifting weights. Yet all the experts agree that any amount of exercise is better than none, and any activity that burns a significant number of calories helps lose body fat and increase the ratio of muscle to fat. The biggest calorie burners are activities like swimming and bicycling, which involve sustained use of large muscle groups in the legs, arms, and torso.

Aerobic exercise—the kind that results in the sustained elevation of both heartbeat and respiration—are thought by some researchers to be best because they also condition the heart and lungs. Running, cross-country skiing, cycling, and swimming are all examples of aerobic exercise.

Strenuous aerobic exercise programs are not feasible for most people on a lifelong basis, however. Jobs and family responsibilities mean that most individuals simply lack the time to be athletes. But a person does not have to live at the gym to be fit. Studies show, for example, that walking can be good aerobic exercise. The U.S. surgeon general recommends thirty minutes a day of physical activity for good health, but that activity can be any one of a number of things—from housework to playing tennis to gardening. Exercise can even be done in small blocks of time that add

Exercise is a key to psychological as well as physical well-being.

up to thirty minutes over the course of the day. Even the kind of fidgeting people do at their desks can add up to a substantial amount of exercise. "The little things we do minute by minute and day by day really do add up,"[60] says Michael Jensen, the leader of a study that revealed that fidgeters burn more calories than nonfidgeters. A stream of nervous movements and a refusal to sit still can burn up as many as seven hundred calories in a day, the equivalent to a six-mile jog.

Even a small amount of exercise carries benefits that go beyond the actual number of calories burned in the process. According to one exercise physiologist, "The key is that when people exercise, no matter how much of it they do, they feel better about themselves. It raises their self-confidence. They feel virtuous. I think when people exercise, the psychological benefits are triggered and that helps them stick to their diet better."[61]

Some researchers believe that exercise leads people to make other healthy decisions: "Exercisers have higher levels of self-esteem and therefore may make better lifestyle choices. If you go for a run in the morning, then you're offered a doughnut later in the day you're more likely to think, 'I've already busted my butt. Why blow it?'"[62]

There is no quick fix to the obesity problem in the United States. Starvation diets, pills, strenuous exercise, and even surgery offer, at best, short-term solutions, but none can be a way of life. Experts recommend a combination of careful eating and sensible, regular exercise as the way to maintain a healthy weight that will contribute to long-term well-being.

Notes

Chapter 1: The Moving Target: Defining Obesity

1. F. Xavier Pi-Sunyer, *Modern Nutrition in Health and Disease*. Philadelphia: Lea & Febiger, 1988, p. 795.

2. Quoted in Lois W. Banner, *American Beauty*. New York: Alfred A. Knopf, 1983, p. 129.

3. Quoted in Banner, *American Beauty*, p. 135.

4. Joan Jacobs Brumberg, *The Body Project: An Intimate History of American Girls*. New York: Random House, 1997, p. 99.

5. Laura Fraser, *Losing It: America's Obsession with Weight and the Industry That Feeds It*. New York: Dutton, 1997, p. 39.

6. Quoted in Fraser, *Losing It*, p. 42.

7. Charles Roy Schroeder, *Fat Is Not a Four-Letter Word*. Minneapolis: Chronimed, 1992, p. 22.

8. Quoted in Karmen Butterer, "The Masculine Mystique," *San Francisco Examiner*, February 28, 1999, p. 20.

9. Mavis Thompson, *The Black Health Library Guide to Obesity*. New York: Henry Holt, 1993, p. 4.

Chapter 2: The Puzzle of Obesity: An Elusive Cause

10. Quoted in Jane Brody, *The New York Times Book of Good Health*. New York: New York Times, 1997, p. 17.

11. Florence Fabricant, "Big Portions Still Make Big People," *New York Times*, October 10, 1994, p. B1.

12. Laura Beil, "Perils of Generation XL," *San Francisco Chronicle*, October 23, 1999, p. 2.

13. Quoted in PlanetRx, "The Rare Truth About Fats," Weightloss2000.com. www.weightloss2000.com/health_library/satis/satis_03_truth.html.

14. Geneen Roth, *When You Eat at the Refrigerator, Pull Up a Chair.* New York: Hyperion, 1998, p. 88.

15. Quoted in Gary Taubes, "As Obesity Rates Rise, Experts Struggle to Explain Why," *Science,* May 29, 1998, p. 1367.

16. Quoted in Beil, "Perils of Generation XL," p. 2.

17. Quoted in Beil, "Perils of Generation XL," p. 2.

18. Quoted in Laura Muha, "Too Fat?" *Parenting,* September 1998, p. 30.

19. Rosemary Green, *Diary of a Fat Housewife.* New York: Warner Books, 1995, p. 267.

20. Sonia Caprio, *The Yale Guide to Children's Nutrition.* New Haven, CT: Yale University Press, 1997, p. 135.

21. Michele Joy Levine, *I Wish I Were Thin, I Wish I Were Fat.* New York: Vanderbilt, 1997, p. 21.

22. Trevor Smith, "And Don't Blame Your Genes for Fat," *Consumers Research Magazine,* February 1996, p. 21.

23. *The PDR Family Guide to Nutrition and Health.* Montvale, NJ: Medical Economics, 1995, p. 82.

24. Smith, "And Don't Blame Your Genes for Fat," p. 22.

25. Quoted in Holly Firfer, "Worried About Weight-Loss? Find Your 'Set Point.'" August 6, 1997. www.diennet.com/goodweight.htm.

26. Smith, "And Don't Blame Your Genes for Fat," p. 22.

27. Sharon Begley, "Shaped by Life in the Womb," *Newsweek*, September 27, 1999, p. 52.

28. *Mayo Clinic Family Health Book.* New York: William Morrow, 1996, p. 288.

Chapter 3: The Consequences of Obesity: More than Just a Health Issue

29. Quoted in *San Francisco Chronicle,* "Obesity Can Cause Early Death, Million-Person Study Confirms," October 7, 1999, p. 2.

30. Quoted in Brody, *The New York Times Book of Health,* p. 80.

31. *The PDR Family Guide to Nutrition and Health,* p. 80.

32. Quoted in Muha, "Too Fat?" p. 131.

33. Blythe Nelson, "Just Fat, Not Stupid," *Radiance,* Spring 1999, p. 17.

34. Quoted in *Overeaters Anonymous.* New York: Overeaters Anonymous, 1980, p. 26.

35. Quoted in Weight Issues, "My Views," April 29, 1999. http://members.aol.com/dbdworld/views.html.

36. Quoted in Weight Issues, "My Views."

37. Quoted in Brody, *The New York Times Book of Health,* p. 44.

Chapter 4: Treating Obesity: Nothing Seems to Work

38. Roth, *When You Eat at the Refrigerator, Pull Up a Chair,* p. 9.

39. Quoted in Maura Rhodes, "America's Top Six Fad Diets," *Good Housekeeping,* July 1996. http://homearts.com:80/gh/health/07nutrf1.htm.

40. Quoted in Michael Fumento, *The Fat of the Land.* New York: Viking, 1997, p. 167.

41. Overeaters Anonymous, "About OA." www.overeatersanonymous.org/about.htm.

Chapter 5: Products and Procedures to Treat Obesity

42. Quoted in Federal Trade Commission, "Commercial Weight Loss Products and Programs: What Consumers Stand to Gain and Lose," October 16–17, 1997. www.ftc.gov/os/1998/9803/weightlo.rpt.htm.

43. Karen Springer, "Finally, the Free Lunch?" *Newsweek,* May 1999, p. 57.

44. Quoted in Overeaters Anonymous, *Overeaters Anonymous,* p. 66.

45. Quoted in William Boggs, "Surgery for Obesity Improves Quality of Life," Reuters Health Information, July 8, 1999. www.obesity.com/news/19990708-213.html.

46. Quoted in Federal Trade Commission, "Commercial Weight Loss Products and Programs."

47. Roth, *When You Eat at the Refrigerator, Pull Up a Chair,* p. 106.

48. Quoted in Federal Trade Commission, "Commercial Weight Loss Products and Programs."

49. Marilyn Wan, telephone interview with the author, June 1999.

Chapter 6: Preventing Obesity

50. Quoted in Brody, *The New York Times Book of Health,* p. 16.

51. Quoted in Michele Meyer, "Eat Less, Do More: The Truth About Losing Body Fat," *Better Homes and Gardens,* March 1999, p. 82.

52. Green, *Diary of a Fat Housewife,* p. 4.

53. Green, *Diary of a Fat Housewife,* p. 45.

54. Roth, *When You Eat at the Refrigerator, Pull Up a Chair,* p. 49.

55. Roth, *When You Eat at the Refrigerator, Pull Up a Chair,* p. 22.

56. Quoted in Beil, "Perils of Generation XL," p. 2.

57. Jerome P. Kassirer, "Losing Weight—an Ill-Fated New Year's Resolution," *New England Journal of Medicine,* January 1, 1998, p. 52.

58. C. Everett Koop, "Crusade to Combat Obesity in America," May 2, 1996. www.shapeup.org/dated/05096.htm.

59. Koop, "Crusade to Combat Obesity in America."

60. Quoted in *San Diego Union-Tribune,* "The Fidget Factor," January 8, 1999, p. 1-A.

61. Quoted in Fumento, *The Fat of the Land,* p. 210.

62. Quoted in Fumento, *The Fat of the Land,* p. 211.

Organizations
to Contact

Federal Trade Commission (FTC)
Correspondence Branch
Washington, DC 20580

The FTC has jurisdiction over advertising and marketing of foods, nonprescription drugs, medical devices, and health care services. It can seek federal court injunctions to halt fraudulent claims and obtain redress for injured consumers.

Food and Drug Administration (FDA)
Consumer Affairs and Information
5600 Fishers Ln.
Rockville, MD 20857

The FDA has jurisdiction over the content and labeling of foods, drugs, and medical devices. It can take legal action to seize and prohibit the sale of products that are falsely labeled.

**National Association to Advance Fat Acceptance
(NAAFA)**
PO Box 188620
Sacramento, CA 95818
(916) 558-6880
fax: (916) 558-6881

NAAFA is a nonprofit human-rights organization dedicated to improving the quality of life for fat people. NAAFA has been working since 1969 to eliminate discrimination based on body size and provide fat people with tools for self-improvement through public education, advocacy, and membership support. NAAFA's Kids Project helps children deal with problems related to weight and body image.

Overeaters Anonymous
World Service Office
6075 Zenith Ct., NE
Rio Rancho, NM 87124
(505) 891-2664
fax: (505) 891-4320

Established in 1960, this worldwide organization follows a twelve-step program to recovery based on abstinence and modeled after the Alcoholics Anonymous program. It has no dues or membership fees and is self-supporting through contributions.

Take Off Pounds Sensibly (TOPS)
4575 South Fifth St.
PO Box 07360
Milwaukee, WI 53207-0360
(414) 482-4620
(800) 932-8677 to locate a chapter

Started in 1948, TOPS is the oldest nonprofit, noncommercial weight-loss program in the United States and Canada. The organization is dedicated to the idea of losing weight sensibly by change of lifestyle and exercise. TOPS tries to help members deal with the underlying causes of overeating through encouragement, support, and education at weekly meetings.

Suggestions for Further Reading

Laura Fraser, *Losing It: America's Obsession with Weight and the Industry That Feeds It.* New York: Dutton, 1997. Fraser examines the history of America's obsession with weight and investigates the weight-loss industry that feeds on and contributes to that obsession.

Michael Fumento, *The Fat of the Land.* New York: Viking, 1997. After reviewing the scientific literature and exploring the factors that contribute to the epidemic of obesity in America, Fumento offers solid advice to people who want to lose weight.

Judith Levine and Linda Bine, *Helping Your Child Lose Weight the Healthy Way.* New York: Carol, 1996. Written in a friendly, up-beat style, this guide provides strategies for concerned parents to help children outgrow their extra weight while building lifelong healthy eating and exercising habits.

Camryn Manheim, *Wake Up, I'm Fat.* New York: Broadway Books, 1999. This memoir by an award-winning actress tells the personal story of a fat girl growing up in a culture obsessed with being thin.

Marilyn Wan, *Fat! So? Because You Don't Have to Apologize for Your Size.* Berkeley, CA: Ten Speed, 1998. Based on an underground magazine by the same name, this light-hearted compendium of essays, true stories, trading cards, paper dolls, and historical facts explores American attitudes toward obesity.

Works Consulted

Books

Michael Anchors, *Safer than Phen-Fen!* Rocklin, CA: Prima, 1997. The author makes claims for the safety of his new appetite-control drug, discusses the nature of obesity, and outlines his plan for safe weight loss.

Nancy C. Baker, *The Beauty Trap: Exploring Woman's Greatest Obsession.* New York: Franklin Watts, 1984. Baker traces the history of women's obsession with physical beauty and offers advice on how to escape this trap.

Lois W. Banner, *American Beauty.* New York: Alfred A. Knopf, New York, 1983. This comprehensive history of the changing concept of beauty in America is enhanced by letters, articles, and anecdotes.

Jane Brody, *The New York Times Book of Good Health.* New York: New York Times, 1997. *New York Times* health columnist Jane Brody has put together a collection of articles, many of which deal with obesity.

Joan Jacobs Brumberg, *The Body Project: An Intimate History of American Girls.* New York: Random House, 1997. Noted historian Joan Brumberg traces the shift from Victorian women's concern with inner beauty to the modern woman's focus on physical appearance, especially the desire to be thin.

Sonia Caprio, *The Yale Guide to Children's Nutrition.* New Haven, CT: Yale University Press, 1997. This text reviews the history, scientific base, and practice of nutrition for students, practitioners, and educators.

Dana K. Cassell, *Encyclopedia of Obesity and Eating Disorders*. New York: Facts On File, 1994. Written for the general reader, this alphabetically arranged encyclopedia offers information on medical and psychological terms, organizations, people associated with eating disorders, and weight-control methods.

Rosemary Green, *Diary of a Fat Housewife*. New York: Warner Books, 1995. The author chronicles her long battle with obesity through comic/tragic diary entries.

Judi Hollis, *Fat Is a Family Affair*. San Francisco: Harper & Row, 1985. This book explores the compulsive nature of eating disorders and the way they affect the entire family.

Michele Joy Levine, *I Wish I Were Thin, I Wish I Were Fat*. New York: Vanderbilt, 1997. A psychiatrist treating patients with weight disorders, Levine discusses the psychological causes of obesity.

Mayo Clinic Family Health Book. New York: William Morrow, 1996. This is a comprehensive medical reference book for use in the home with information on diseases, exercise, and nutrition.

Susie Orbach, *Fat Is a Feminist Issue . . . the Anti-Diet Guide to Permanent Weight Loss*. New York: Paddington, 1978. Considered a classic of feminist literature, this book shows women how to break the cycle of diet and weight gain by adopting a nondicting approach to weight loss through self-acceptance.

Overeaters Anonymous. New York: Overeaters Anonymous, 1980. This collection of first-person narratives by Overeaters Anonymous members chronicles their battles with compulsive overeating.

The PDR Family Guide to Nutrition and Health. Montvale, NJ: Medical Economics, 1995. A medical resource for the layperson.

F. Xavier Pi-Sunyer, *Modern Nutrition in Health and Disease*. Philadelphia: Lea & Febiger, 1988. This authoritative resource answers dozens of questions regarding children's nutrition and provides recipes from famous chefs for delicious and healthy dishes.

Geneen Roth, *When You Eat at the Refrigerator, Pull Up a Chair.* New York: Hyperion, 1998. A witty, personal history of the author's struggle with obesity.

Charles Roy Schroeder, *Fat Is Not a Four-Letter Word.* Minneapolis: Chronimed, 1992. This witty, information-filled story of fat covers history, science, treatment, and an indictment against the American diet industry.

William Tamberlane, ed., *The Yale Guide to Children's Nutrition.* New Haven, CT: Yale University Press, 1997. This authoritative resource covers a range of topics dealing with childhood nutrition, including childhood obesity.

Mavis Thompson, *The Black Health Library Guide to Obesity.* New York: Henry Holt, 1993. Dr. Thompson provides information on many aspects of obesity and their importance for African Americans in particular.

U.S. Department of Health and Human Services, *The Surgeon General's Report on Nutrition and Health.* Washington, DC: GPO, 1988. A comprehensive health resource written in fairly technical language.

Naomi Wolf, *The Beauty Myth: How Images of Beauty Are Used Against Women.* New York: William Morrow, 1991. Feminist Naomi Wolf examines the unrealistic standards of female beauty that have been created by the media, diet, fashion, and cosmetic industries and used against women as a destructive form of social control.

The Yale Guide to Children's Nutrition. New Haven, CT: Yale University Press, New Jersey, 1997. An excellent resource for information about children's nutrition for home use.

Periodicals

Sharon Begley, "Shaped by Life in the Womb," *Newsweek,* September 27, 1999.

Laura Beil, "Perils of Generation XL," *San Francisco Chronicle,* October 23, 1999.

Karmen Butterer, "The Masculine Mystique," *San Francisco Examiner,* February 28, 1999.

Geoffrey Cowley and Karen Springer, "Lowdown on Liposuction," *Newsweek,* May 24, 1999.

Florence Fabricant, "Big Portions Still Make Big People," *New York Times,* October 10, 1994.

Harvard Health Letter, "Guidelines Call More Americans Overweight," August 1998.

Mindy Herman, "Lose Weight Faster," *Family Circle,* November 1, 1999.

Jerome P. Kassircr, "Losing Weight—an Ill-Fated New Year's Resolution," *New England Journal of Medicine,* January 1, 1998.

Susan Kano, "Making Peace with Food," National Association to Advance Fat Acceptance, 1999.

Lifetimes, "Loving the Body You Live In," Summer 1999.

Thomas H. Maugh II, "Americans Getting Fatter Fast—Hormone Study Offers Hope," *San Francisco Chronicle,* October 27, 1999.

Michelle Meyer, "Eat Less, Do More: The Truth About Losing Body Fat," *Better Homes and Gardens,* March 1999.

Laura Muha, "Too Fat?" *Parenting,* September 1998.

Blythe Nelson, "Just Fat, Not Stupid," *Radiance,* Spring 1999.

New York Times, "Most Americans Are Overweight," October 16, 1996.

———, "Race Can Affect Rate of Obesity," March 26, 1997.

Jamie Reno and John Leland, "Heavy Meddling," *Newsweek,* October 18, 1999.

Kathryn Rose et al. "What Determines Waist-Hip Ration and Waist Circumference in Women Twins?" *Nutrition Research Newsletter,* February 1999.

Michael Rosenbaum and Rudolph L. Leibel, "The Physiology of Body Weight Regulation: Relevance to the Etiology of Obesity in Children." (The Causes and Health Consequences of Obesity in Children and Adolescents), *Pediatrics,* March 1998.

San Diego Union-Tribune, "The Fidget Factor," January 8, 1999.

San Francisco Chronicle, "Obesity Can Cause Early Death, Million-Person Study Confirms," October 7, 1999.

————, "Teen Diet Heavy in Chips, Fries, Research Finds," October 27, 1999.

————, "Weight-Loss Firms Agree to Federal Guidelines," February 10, 1999.

Trevor Smith, "And Don't Blame Your Genes for Fat," *Consumers Research Magazine,* February 1996.

Karen Springer, "Finally, the Free Lunch?" *Newsweek,* May 1999.

————, "Making Calories Count," *Newsweek,* Spring/Summer 1999.

Sheryl Gay Stolberg, "FDA Approves Diet Drug That Blocks Fat Absorption," *San Francisco Chronicle,* April 27, 1999.

Gary Taubes, "As Obesity Rates Rise, Experts Struggle to Explain Why," *Science,* May 29, 1998.

I. A. Sorenson Thorkild, "Leptin," British Medicine Association, 1996.

John Travis, "Genes Induce Human Obesity," *Science News,* June 28, 1997.

Michelle Puelia Turk, "Is There a Diet Drug for You?" *USA Weekend,* May 21, 1999.

Internet Sources

Better Business Bureau, "Weight Loss Promotions," 1995. www.bosbbb.org/lit/0147.htm.

Michael Blumenkrantz, "Obesity: The World's Oldest Metabolic Disorder," 1997. www.quantumhcp.com/ obesity. htm.

William Boggs, "Surgery for Obesity Improves Quality of Life," Reuters Health Information, July 8, 1999. www.obesity. com/news/19990708-213.html.

Doctor's Guide, "New Study Examines Demographic and Cultural Links to Obesity," March 4, 1997. www.pslgroup.com/ docguide.htm.

Federal Trade Commission, "Commercial Weight Loss Products and Programs: What Consumers Stand to Gain and Lose," October 16–17, 1997. www.ftc.gov/os/1998/9803/ weightlo.rpt.htm.

Holly Firfer, "Worried About Weight-Loss? Find Your 'Set Point.'" August 6, 1997. www.diennet.com/goodweight. htm.

Chuck Forsberg, "Adiposity 101," 1997. www.rdrop.com/ users/caf/adipos.html.

Lisa Hark and Lisa Stollman, "The Reincarnation of the High Protein Diet," October 10, 1997. www.heartinfo.org/ nutrition/hprotein101097.htm.

C. Everett Koop, "Crusade to Combat Obesity in America," May 2, 1996. www.shapeup.org/dated/05096.htm.

Michael Myers, "Frequently Asked Medication Questions." www.weight.com/faqmed.html.

National Association to Advance Fat Acceptance, "NAAFA Information Index." www.naafa.org/documents/brochures/ naafa-info.html.

Overeaters Anonymous, "About OA." www.overeatersanonymous.org/about.htm.

PlanetRx, "The Rare Truth About Fats," Weightloss2000.com. www.weightloss2000.com/health_library/satis/satis_03_ truth.html.

Maura Rhodes, "America's Top Six Fad Diets," *Good Housekeeping*, July 1996. http://homearts.com:80/gh/health /07nutrf1.htm.

Take Off Pounds Sensibly, "Facts About TOPS." www.tops.org/html/information.html.

Thrive Online, "Basic Diet Plans." www.thriveonline.com/weight/diets/types1.html.

Weight Issues, "My Views," April 29, 1999. http://members.aol.com/dbdworld/views.html.

Index

Picture Credits

About the Author

Charlene Ackers was born in New York City and grew up in Berkeley, California. She received a bachelor's degree and a master's degree in Spanish and a Candidacy in Philosophy in Comparative Literature from the University of California at Berkeley.

Ms. Akers has written several non-fiction books including *Never Buy Anything New Except This Book*, *Open to the Public*, *First and Foremost*, and the introduction to *920 O'Farrell Street*. She has one son, Ryan and lives in San Francisco with her husband Nate Levine and their two poodles, Charley and Lexie.